Happy
ever after?

**A Practical Guide to Relationship
Counselling for Clinical Psychologists**

Bruce Stevens and Malise Arnstein

www.
AUSTRALIANACADEMIC**PRESS**
.com.au

First published in 2011
Australian Academic Press
32 Jeays Street
Bowen Hills Qld 4006
Australia
www.australianacademicpress.com.au

National Library of Australia Cataloguing-in-Publication entry:

Author:	Stevens, Bruce A., 1950-
Title:	Happy ever after? : a practical guide to relationship counselling for clinical psychologists / Bruce Stevens and Malise Arnstein.
Edition:	1st ed.
ISBN:	9781921513794 (pbk.)
Subjects:	Couples therapy. Psychotherapy. Clinical sociology.
Other Authors/Contributors:	
	Arnstein, Malise.
Dewey Number:	616.891562

Contents

Acknowledgments v

Chapter 1
Introduction: Clinical psychology and relationship counselling 1

Chapter 2
Historical perspective, including systems theory 5

Chapter 3
The first interview and initial assessment 11

Chapter 4
The assessment of the relationship, including conflict 21

Chapter 5
Emotional processes underlying relationship conflict.................... 45

Chapter 6
The sexual affair 59

Chapter 7
Sex therapy: The scope and the challenges 77

Chapter 8
When personality disorder adds to relationship problems............ 95

Chapter 9
Additional considerations: Different happy couples....................... 121

Chapter 10
Self-psychology and couples therapy: The building blocks 135
for a focus on couple inter-affectivity

Appendix
Family-of-Origin scale 169

Endnotes... 173

References... 175

Acknowledgments

I want to thank my co-author Malise Arnstein. We have written different sections and she has drawn on areas of specialist expertise that I lack. She contributed Chapter 7 on sex therapy, the domestic violence section at the end of Chapter 8, the therapy with gay and lesbian couples section of Chapter 9 and Chapter 10 on self-psychology. I wrote the rest of the book.

I would like to express my appreciation to my students in the clinical program at the University of Canberra, and other students and supervisees who have sharpened my clinical thinking. I also appreciate what workshop participants have added over the past 10 years, especially related to personality disorder. I have a wonderful family, Jennie (we have been married 38 years) and our four adult children: Rowena with Christian, Kym with Marty, Naomi, Christopher with Carol. Rowena and Christian have two children, so the next generation of the Stevens family is in good hands!

— Bruce Stevens, PhD

I want to express my thanks to Bruce Stevens, PhD, my long-term colleague and friend, who finally managed to get me to do some writing. Without his initiative, energy, encouragement and insistence I would have never been a co-author of any book.

My gratitude also goes to Jac Brown, PhD, in Sydney, without whose work on gay and lesbian couples my section on this topic would have not been possible. Similarly, I would like to thank the management committee of the Canberra Marriage Counselling Centre (now Relationships Australia ACT) for hiring me as Assistant Director of the agency in 1981 just after I married and

18 months after I moved to Australia. I want to thank all my teachers; in particular, Luigi Boscolo, MD, Laurie MacKinnon, PhD, Kerrie James, MA, Ron Lee, PhD, Robert Gordon, MD, Keryl Egan, MA, and Tom Young, PhD. I would also like to thank my supervisors, colleague, clients, family and friends for sharing their knowledge and life experience with me over the years. They all contributed in unique ways to my understanding of relationships and to the motivation to learn more and more about couples and how to help intimate partners to feel better about themselves and live more satisfying lives either together or apart. Finally, I want to thank John Hutchinson, PhD (Mathematics), my partner of over 30 years, for sharing our personal journey, the ups and downs of joint domesticity and two careers in very diverse fields. He has been a great source of support as a model of academic enthusiasm and discipline, as well as a reliable and pedantic editor.

— Malise Arnstein, PhD

Chapter 1

Introduction: Clinical psychology and relationship counselling

Much relationship counselling today is conducted by generalist psychologists, social workers, and counsellors; yet there is a strong case for a greater role for clinical psychologists. Accurate assessment during couples therapy is essential; the dynamics between people are complex, and the process is potentially very demanding of clinical skills. The purpose of this text is to provide an opportunity to make the argument for greater involvment in relationship counselling by the clinical psychology profession and to guide both clinical and counselling students on the necessary skills for effective treatment.

A clinical psychologist, like a psychiatrist, is well trained in the diagnosis of disorder, and relationship issues are often related to psychological disorders and comorbid conditions. Consider the following three scenarios.

Mary has brought Mark, recently returned from war service in Afghanistan, into counselling because of concerns for his gambling and how much it is costing the family. Is his military service playing some role in the increase in his gambling?

Kylie has a problem with her anger. Brett is threatening to leave if her aggression is not better contained. Is her irritability that of an untreated depression or perhaps the brooding anger of a borderline personality disorder?

Bettina is taking lithium for bipolar disorder and has just come out of hospital after a two-week admission related to her anorexia, and there is a need to closely monitor her weight. Natalie, her partner, is feeling highly stressed. She loves Bet, but feels overwhelmed by a responsibility to keep her alive. What support and guidance is best for Bettina?

It is clear that while there are relationship issues with these three couples there are also psychological disorders, which add to a complex clinical presentation. It is important to have a good understanding of disorders such as addiction, posttraumatic stress disorder (PTSD), depression, borderline personality disorder, anorexia and bipolar disorder. We can also think about how such disorders might impact an intimate relationship. Perhaps it is to state the obvious, but such potential complexity demands greater clinical training — not less!

This is also a field in which relationship myths can dominate treatment, often for decades, and there is an urgent need for clarity of thought which comes through research. Our work as clinical psychologists needs to be informed by the best evidence-based treatment (EBT). Only this will effectively guide the couples or individuals we might treat with relationship issues. At times it may be necessary to be able to offer individual sessions and then coordinate with the work of relationship counselling. For example, Mark, with a gambling problem, might have treatment with motivational interviewing. But first, should there be an assessment for PTSD? An effective treatment can be planned with the couple, perhaps drawing on the strengths of both, but this is best carried out by a mental health professional thoroughly versed in diagnostic and treatment experience. Additionally, some mental health problems follow the dissolution of an important relationship.

Not all relationship problems come from psychological or personality disorders; many are the result of differing needs in the relationship. There may also be dysfunctional patterns and features of personality that defy change. In this book we will rely heavily on the research and recommendations of clinical psychologist Dr John Gottman, a leading researcher and clinician in this area. His 'Love Lab' has provided years of data on couple processes that can helpfully inform our practice, with easy-to-understand principles thoroughly grounded in extensive research. While there has not yet been randomised, controlled trial (RCT) evidence from Gottman and his colleagues, I believe his work would meet the criteria of the American Psychological Association's (APA) policy statement on evidence-based practice in psychology (EBPP): '... the integration of the best available research with clinical expertise in the context of patient characteristics, culture, and preferences' (see APA, 2006).

Sexton and Gordon (2009) distinguished three levels:

1. Evidence-informed interventions based on pre-existing evidence.

2. Promising interventions but preliminary results not replicated.

3. Evidence-based treatments with systematic high quality evidence demonstrating that efficacy with clinical problems the interventions are designed to address.

In his keynote address to the 27th International Congress of Applied Psychology, James Bray (2010) said that there is some level 3 support for the following therapeutic approaches: behavioural marital therapy (Jacobson & Margolin, 1979), cognitive–behavour therapy (CBT) marital therapy (Baucom & Epstein, 1990), integrative couple therapy (Jacobson & Christensen, 1996), and emotion-focused couples therapy (EFT-C; Greenberg & Goldman, 2008). EFT-C has strong links to attachment theory. I will introduce this approach and commend it as worthy of practical application in the treatment of couples.

I remember an era when the basic assumption of relationship counselling was to encourage a couple to communicate as someone in therapy might talk to their psychologist; however, the reality is that this is too difficult for most couples to achieve, and not even typical of how happily married people tend to communicate! I wrote a couple of books based on this premise, and I am pleased to have this opportunity to update practice in light of more recent research.

It is clear that there are important skills in relationship counselling, and many clinical psychologists in practice might lack both confidence and skills for this work. But this should change because clinical psychologists have something important to offer, with a potentially more informed and integrated approach to relationship counselling, drawing on the best evidence-based treatments. And as a final thought, as clinical psychologists, as we have proven ourselves competent in research, we can possibly lead the way in finding more effective ways to treat patients in difficult relationships characterised by significant psychopathology and personality disorder.

> **To do**
>
> I would encourage reading these texts:
>
> Gottman, J. (1999). *The marriage clinic: A scientifically based marital therapy.* New York: W.W. Norton.
>
> Gottman, J., & Silver, N. (1999). *The seven principles for making a marriage work.* New York: Three Rivers Press.
>
> Greenberg, L.S., & Goldman, R.N. (2008). *Emotion-focused couples therapy: The dynamics of emotion, love and power.* Washington, DC: American Psychological Association.
>
> Johnson, S.M. (2004). The practice of emotionally focused couple therapy: Creating connection. New York: Brunner Routledge.

It would be very helpful to read the first text listed above and draw on the research, exercises and questionnaires in the appendices in your work with couples. This text is quite comprehensive. I would recommend having a number of copies of the second text (Gottman & Silver, 1999) to loan to couples in treatment, or encourage them to get their own copy. The third text (Greenberg & Goldman, 2008) is a comprehensive introduction to EFT-C, the leading EBT in relationship therapy. And last is Johnson (2004) which is the most practical guide for a couple therapist. I consider this text essential reading, and the most important I have read for working with couples. I will introduce and cover some of its main ideas in the following chapters.

Chapter 2

Historical perspective, including systems theory

There is a moment in an Anglican service of marriage when the priest takes the hand of the bride from her father and 'gives her' to the husband-to-be. This is a symbol of 'property transfer'. While this is understandably offensive to our modern understanding, it is a relic of a former age when marriage was primarily about material possessions. It is only since the 17th century that political, economic and cultural change in Europe began to erode the older functions of marriage by 'encouraging individuals to choose their mates on the basis of personal affection and allowing couples to challenge the rights of outsiders to intrude upon their lives' (Coontz, 2006, p. 7). The idea of romantic love is relatively recent and arguably a less stable foundation for marriage. One thing is certain, that idealism in relation to relationships can only add to the need for relationship counselling.

Historical outline of relationship therapy

The early practitioners of marriage counselling were medical doctors, including physician-sexologists, gynaecologists, and psychiatrists, as well as educators, lawyers, social workers and clergy. The rise of the profession began with counselling centres such as Abraham and Hannah Stone's New York City Clinic (1929), and Paul Popenoe's American Institute of Family Relations in Los Angeles (1930). The American Association for Marriage Counsellors was formed in 1942.

Some psychoanalysts who worked with individuals in troubled relationships became frustrated with the lack of change in marriage and family patterns. This led to an interest in general systems theory. The focus became patterns of interactive behaviour rather than the personalities of individual people. Significant advances came in the 1950s. Psychiatrist Murray Bowen's study in schizophrenia was very influential. He understood the family unit as the focus of the problem (von Bertalanffy, 1968; Werner, 1957). Also Gregory Bateson, a social scientist, was interested in schizophrenia and proposed the 'double bind' theory. Nathan Ackerman was interested in family psychiatry. Other leaders included Virginia Satir, Carl Whittaker, Sal Minuchin, and the pioneers of the Milan school. In recent decades Australian social worker Michael White developed an original and effective style of therapy, which has been recognised internationally.[1] I have found the research of John Gottman about couple distress highly informative, and the treatment principles of emotion-focused couples therapy (EFT-C) enormously valuable.

Systems theory

If we are to think about more than symptoms, then it is valuable to have some kind of theory that tries to explain the complexity of relationships and family dynamics. Historically, most approaches have drawn on systems concepts. This describes what happens in terms of the whole and not the various parts. It is difficult to grasp the principles because we tend to think in terms of linear causation: A leads to B to C, and so on. Systems theory is more dynamic and interactional: *Imagine five marbles in the lid of a coffee jar. On one level the marbles interact in linear terms but if the lid is moved then there is an effect on all the marbles at the same time.* In systems thought, components are seen as behaving in terms of their position in the network, rather than according to their nature. There is a recognition that each component may well function in a different way outside the system.

Systems theory better describes the dynamic quality of families. This theory has led to a therapeutic approach that has a focus on systemic forces rather than the specific content of symptoms.

One systems concept is triangles, which has a broader relevance than the 'eternal triangle' of the marital affair. *A psychologist explained the bad behaviour of a teenager as an attempt to hold the parents' marriage together: 'After all, the only time that I have ever seen you two agree is when you condemn what Bobby has done!'*

I have found that a thorough understanding of one approach to marital therapy is helpful in counselling couples. It brings depth and coherence to couple work. Techniques can then be drawn from various other approaches and integrated without therapeutic confusion. I have no particular ideological commitment to any of the schools of thought, it is more a question of style, although I would slightly favour the therapy with the best evidence base — currently EFT-C — which was informed by systems theory. However, any of the main theorists in marital counselling can provide a comprehensive map for working with couples.

Introduction to the thought of Murray Bowen

There are different theoretical approaches to relationship counselling and family therapy. I will illustrate a systems approach by using the thought of Murray Bowen. His work has influenced a number of leading practitioners such as David Schnarch (1997), who has written extensively in sex therapy, and Lerner (1989). While a systems theory does not always play a major part in contemporary approaches to couple therapy, it is valuable to understand historically and to better appreciate what was to follow.

Bowen trained as a psychiatrist and had a position on the staff of the Menninger Clinic from 1946 to 1954. He noticed that he could think more objectively about the patients on the ward when he was away from the clinic. This insight led to his conceptualisation of groups of people as an emotional field and the family as an 'emotional unit'. The field regulates the attitudes and behaviour of the members to varying degrees. He also began to appreciate that the functioning of a family was more understandable when considered in the context of the multigenerational past. After a particularly tense time with his own family he applied his theory to his own struggles and shared the results at a national meeting of family therapists in 1967 (Anonymous, 1972).

According to Bowen, every person has some degree of unresolved *emotional attachment* to his family. This relates to Bowen's concept of *differentiation of self*. The level of differentiation can be equated to the capacity to say 'I' when others are demanding 'you' or 'we'. Differentiation also describes the ability of an individual to maintain emotional autonomy in a relationship system. But autonomy is not synonymous with isolation. Bowen understood that the higher the level of self, the greater the ability not only to maintain a self in relationship to others, but also to permit others to be themselves. The lower the differentiation of self, the more intense is a person's emotional need for others to think, feel, and behave in certain ways. The lower the level of basic differentiation, the more tendency there is to 'borrow' self from others to shore up the level of functioning (Kerr, 1984, p. 9).

Reflect

1. Think of a person who you would identify as emotionally mature and self-directed in their choices in life. What are their most obvious characteristics? What is it about them that you admire?

2. Think of a person who is very immature. Do they have difficulty making up their mind and staying with a course of action? Are they influenced too much by parents and friends? Are decisions made by impulse or hastily made in an emotional state?

By reflecting on the two types of people you have indentified as emotionally 'mature' and 'immature', you can begin to distinguish between high and low self-differentiation.

A lack of differentiation leads to relationships characterised by *emotional intensity* and *reactivity*. The family of origin is relevant because the adult's level of differentiation largely depends on the degree of differentiation attained while growing up in the family system.

The character of unresolved emotional attachment takes many forms. It can range from an intense and conflictual relationship to an overly idealised, harmonious bond. The critical issue is how much the feelings, thinking, and behaviour of each person is regulated by emotional forces in the relationship (Kerr, 1984, p. 11). The mood is of secondary importance. One of the therapeutic goals of this approach is to work on change in the self while maintaining contact with the important people in the *family of origin*. Unresolved tension in a family can lead to the development of symptoms. As Michael Kerr (1988) explained: 'It is easier for the family members to make accommodations that make it possible to live with the symptom than it is to address the underlying relationship process that fosters the symptom in the first place' (p. 57).

Another important concept is *emotional distance*. The two extremes are 'fused' relationships and 'emotional cut-offs'. Both are motivated by a lack of differentiation. Distancing may be the result of a lack of emotional space in the relationship. Friedman (1985) observed that partners may separate because they have grown distant, but most couples probably separate because they are not able to achieve any separation at all. A more *well-defined self* is able to balance these emotional forces.

Emotional cut-offs can be seen in terms of physical distance. For example:

> A patient's father died in a local nursing home. The father, in his thirties, left his wife and three young children. He lived with a de facto partner and had two children to her — one was the patient I saw. He only saw his original family once in the next 10 years, though some of his children regained contact when he was placed in a nursing home after a severe accident. There was some discomfort at the funeral that was attended by both families, which the father had kept separate with his emotional cut-off.

Emotional cut-offs can also be an internal state when an individual withdraws into television, books, fantasy, alcohol, drugs, or depression. Such cut-offs raise anxiety and shift problems onto other people in the family system. This emotional dynamic adds to many of the difficulties that occur in second marriages or blended families.

Differentiation happens *in* relationships with significant others. Little difference would occur if a patient suddenly went to live in Antarctica for a year as this would be an emotional cut-off. The important balance to try to achieve in a relationship is emotional connection, while retaining some capacity for autonomy. Naturally this can be difficult to achieve — but that is a healthy emotional goal for any relationship.

There has been an artificial distinction of the medical model and systems-based therapies. The two approaches, while different, are not mutually exclusive. One of the challenges for clinical psychologists who do relationship counselling will be to move more freely between different schools of thought. I think it is also important for clinical psychology to be interested in models of personality that offer depth, such as dynamic theories, and more systemic understandings. In this way, theory and practice can come together in ways that facilitate therapeutic work.

This chapter has provided something of an historical perspective, with an introduction to systems theory. See also the Family-of-Origin scale in the Appendix. In the next chapter I will look at the conducting the first interview and begin the process of assessment, which is foundational to treatment.

Chapter 3

The first interview and initial assessment

The first interview begins with initial contact. Generally the more motivated (or anxious) person will ring and arrange the first session. An exception is when one of the couple has decided to leave the relationship and wants to leave the abandoned partner with a caretaker (i.e., the psychologist). Such agendas are not always obvious.

The first meeting will give a number of clues that can be meaningful. How do they greet you? First name? Formally, with Mr, Ms, or Dr? Or 'We have come to you as a shrink'. This will indicate something of the relationship expected. Where do they choose to sit? In my office there are three or four chairs. Couples who come for premarital guidance inevitably sit together (holding hands); those in marital distress sit as far apart as the room allows! Generally I find that the one who arranged the interview will sit closer to me — implying that they have found an ally.

Often one person is reluctant to enter into counselling or has already made up their mind to leave the relationship. In terms of presentation, this person can be seen as having more power, as he or she will have less need of the relationship. If there is to be any effective treatment then it is a matter of the highest priority to engage that distancing person. Only in this way can you achieve a meaningful 'working alliance'. They are usually easy to pick and I make sure that I give that person considerable attention, affirm their perspective and try to be empathic to the pain they have experienced. Naturally, I will also listen and try to understand their partner as well. A shared sense of understanding is essential for there to be any possibility for a second interview. Sometimes both will want to work on the presenting problem and it is a good prognostic sign. Occasionally both individuals will want to end the relationship and they can be helped to part with a minimum of hurt to themselves and their children.

If possible, schedule 60 to 90 minutes for the first appointment if you know it is couple counselling. Medicare rebates a maximum of 50 minutes with a mental health care plan. Treatment is limited to interpersonal psychotherapy, which it may be appropriate to one or both as part of the treatment process. Working with couples is listed as a treatment for depressed patients. Usually some time is needed to make a preliminary assessment (described later).

Towards the end of the first interview I will give about 3 minutes to each to be alone with me and I will ask: 'Is there anything that you can only say to me without your partner being here?'. I may then be told about violence or alcohol abuse or some 'dark secret'. I always ask a specific question about whether there is or has been an affair. It is a powerful secret that has an influence on the progress of therapy. Usually this is answered truthfully, but not always. Another useful question is: 'Is there anything I should know in order to help you?'. You may also want to see each person individually for a session to get a more extensive picture of how they both see the relationship. This can be helpful, but ensure that the number of individual sessions is balanced (make sure you have at least one with the partner and offer for an equal number).

In the first session a couple will demonstrate their fighting style. This is a source of valuable 'here and now' information. Is the couple out of control, sarcastic, mutual in their blame, verging on violence, passive, silent? Sometimes there are clear roles: one may be submissive while the other is aggressive and overbearing. Any expression of conflict may be taboo, with the result that there is great reluctance to address any issue directly. It is informative to see what attempts are made to move from being stuck. This will usually reveal a limited range of coping styles and a restricted capacity to adapt. How do the people in the relationship try to repair? It is especially important to note whether there is a 'harsh start-up'.

Another question to keep in mind is 'Why now?'. Usually something has led to the decision to seek help. Has it been a severe fight, an affair, a decision to leave, or suicidal thoughts? If there are significant comorbid conditions then it may be wise to work in tandem with a psychiatrist, an outpatient unit or an agency (e.g., with alcohol dependence).

You will want to check with the couple as to their expectations of treatment. What would they like to see happen? How do they see counselling helping? In this way you can tailor treatment to their felt needs and what they might expect to work for them in their relationship. There is outcome research that implies this approach has the best treatment results (Hubble, Duncan, & Miller, 1999).

It is helpful to give some indication of how long treatment might take: 'I would like to see you both for six sessions. You may well see some improvement by then and we can re-assess'. I also try to give an impression of how I see the problem and propose a way forward. For example:

> One couple was worried about violence in their relationship. Every 18 months or so they had a fight that got out of control. The last one ended up with more than bruises. I normalised conflict with the comment: 'If you fight that rarely, then it is amazing that you haven't killed each other!' and explained that they would need to learn to fight more often, but with more focus and learn some skills for containing destructive emotional expression.

The act of coming to see a psychologist can be reassuring and a source of hope. But progress needs to be made quickly if both people are to remain engaged in the work of therapy.

This work will draw on all your skills of counselling such as empathic listening and dealing with intense emotions. Therapy is not passive, working with couples tends to be active: clarifying, refereeing, asking questions, teaching communication skills and assigning homework tasks. It is enormously important to learn the role of emotions in the relationship. I encourage the couple to take increasing responsibility for their progress and affirm useful initiatives they might undertake. I model listening and interpersonal respect, which is one way of demonstrating communication skills. Gottman (1999) noted the difficulties in relationship counselling, including high relapse rate, but added: 'Anything we do will work to some degree, as long as the therapist is highly active and the intervention has some clear rationale that is articulated ... otherwise, people will terminate against professional advice' (p. 6). However to advance beyond this, it is necessary to 'give science a chance'.

Important don'ts

1. *Don't take sides.* The psychologist should not be seduced into siding with one person, but empathise with both without losing a stance of neutrality, while maintaining a relationship or systems perspective. Sometimes it helps to keep shifting back and forth to try to understand from multiple perspectives. I find it safest to be an advocate for the relationship not either party and this is appropriate while both are willing for it to continue. A sign that this stance is working is when both partners suspect that you are slightly more on the other's side.

2. *Don't intervene too quickly.* It is best to go slow and cautiously act in ways that are safe to the couple. Be curious.

3. *Don't answer questions from the couple until you are ready.* Say 'That is a good question. Can we hold it until a bit later?'

4. *Don't proceed until you have some understanding of the problem and goals for treatment.* Say: 'Based on what you have said so far, my initial impression is ...'

5. *Don't discuss problems in the abstract.* Ask questions that lead to concrete responses: 'You say that she dismisses you. What would be a recent example?'

6. *Don't discount problems, even the seemingly trivial.* These may be important to one or both and have highly symbolic meanings for the relationship.

7. *Don't allow conflict to escalate in a session.* See the intensity and investment in the issue but then set boundaries to dampen the interaction. Emotion can easily dominate a session and erode goodwill.

8. *Don't get hooked into the past.* Present interactions should give you enough to proceed.

9. *Don't listen endlessly to either partner's explanations of the problems.* Watch giving too much permission to tell stories as this can waste valuable time.

10. *Don't allow the couple to take charge of the session* (Weeks & Treat, 1992, pp. 4–8).

Note that neutrality — that is, not taking sides — is extremely difficult. Sometimes one or other will be completely unreasonable in what is asked. If you are to confront this make sure that you balance it by confronting the other partner on something that might be unrealistically expected.

There is usually one point of common ground in all couples presenting for treatment. Both will blame the other for problems in the relationship and possibly believe that they would be happy if only some aspects of their partner's character could change.

Gottman (1999) has many assessment resources, including the Clinician's Checklist for Marital Assessment, Locke-Wallace Marital Adjustment test, Weiss-Cerreto Marital Status Inventory, Symptom Checklist 90 (SCL-90), Conflict Tactics scales (CTS), Waltz-Rushe-Gottman Emotional Abuse Questionnaire (EAQ), Gottman Love and Respect scale, Gottman Marital Style Questionnaire, the Distance and Isolation Questionnaires, Gottman Areas of Disagreement scale, Gottman Areas of Change Checklist, Gottman 17 Areas scale, Gottman Areas of Strengths

Checklist and the Sound Marital House Questionnaires. All of these are published in Gottman's *The Marriage Clinic* and can be used in clinical practice and research.

The genogram

It has been said that being born into a family is like arriving three hours late for a party. Much of the action is past tense.

The genogram is a simple way of organising information about families over three generations. It was developed in family therapy, but is now far more widely used. I find it essential in assessment and in general it is the part of my notes that I most 'keep my eye on'. It is also helpful to keep track of family members and to maintain an intergenerational systems perspective.

The following details are usually included on the diagram:

- names, age, highest level of education, occupation, and significant problems
- dates of birth, death, marriages, divorces, separations (anniversaries tend to raise anxiety or cause sadness), any other significant stressors or transitions, including: accidents, illness, change of job, moving house; especially note these if any have occurred just before a legally relevant event such as work related stress, separation or an injury
- geographical locations of parents and other family members, patterns of migration
- ethnic and religious affiliations.

These details provide the bones of the genogram. The flesh is the emotional patterns. This can include such themes as alcohol abuse, addictions, genetic defects, suicide, violence, accidents, job instability, problems with gambling, sexual abuse, criminal behaviour, drug addiction and mental illness (all of which should be checked). Who are the success stories in the family? What are the criteria (business, academic, sport, or financial success)? Are there clear gender roles? How important are sibling positions? Who are the 'black sheep' or 'scapegoats'? What are the family rules, taboos, hot issues, secrets, and family scripts?

It is also interesting to consider the historical forces that shaped each generation. What wars, economic conditions, birth-rate changes, cultural forces and new technologies were influential? Have notions about gender changed or remained the same? If there was a migration, what differences in culture were intro-duced? One cultural value that influences self-care is selflessness versus self-consideration. Did this change in the family? How has the meaning of work changed through the generations? Note that the genogram is a tool in which you can create your own symbols to track what you want in a clinical history.

The genogram in Figure 3.1 shows that both Tom and Nancy grew up in alcoholic homes. Nancy lives much closer to her immediate family and tends to get involved in their dramas. In 1986, the year after the stillbirth of her daughter, she had multiple stresses following the death of her mother: her father increased his drinking and her younger brother was admitted to

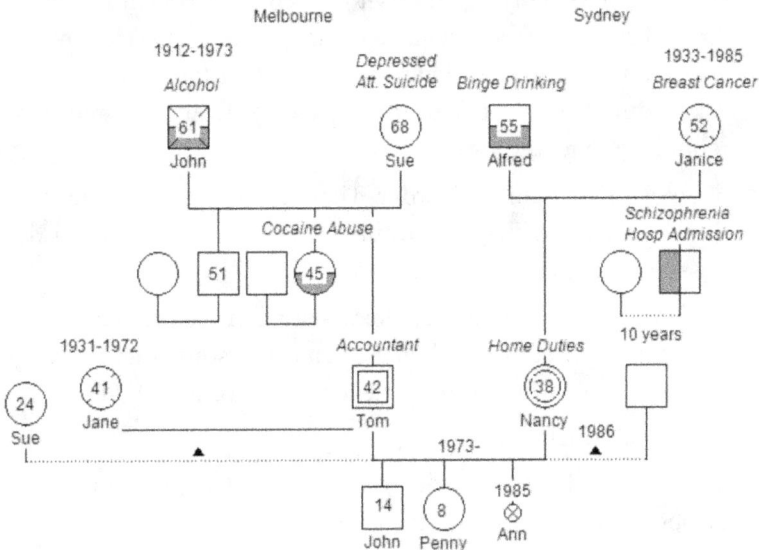

FIGURE 3.1
A genogram.

hospital with a diagnosis of schizophrenia. This might explain her need for additional support, which she sought in the brief affair with Joe. Tom and Nancy are now presenting for relationship counselling because she is 'having feelings' for a man who volunteers for tuckshop duty. She complains that Tom works long hours, neglects his family and household tasks.

Practical application

There are many practical applications for the genogram; it can assist you to:

- keep track of people, the situation, and context of the relationship. It is easier to focus on a visual diagram (and return to where everything is summarised) than scribbled notes.

- place the symptom in context. We can see family history, which might be important to distinguish a biological from a reactive depression. This leads to a more accurate diagnosis. I once saw a military couple with an 18-year-old daughter, who initially I thought was being rebellious, but in the next session I found that the maternal grandmother was bipolar. I then had to consider the possibility of an onset of a chronic mental illness. A lot of disorders have a genetic contribution. Antisocial behaviour, violence, and addictions run through families. You can ask about these in a matter-of-fact way. Doing a genogram reminds you to ask the questions.

- diagnose personality disorder. There are usually intergenerational patterns of neglect, trauma and abuse which raise the possibility of personality vulnerability.

- see problems in a larger context. With complex families with strong intergenerational themes, you can assume that recovery will take longer. This is also true for relationship difficulties.

- track emotional themes.

- use it as a flexible tool so that you can create your own symbols for whatever interests you.

- easily track relationship quality over the generations — what parents modelled to children — and consider patterns of nurture.

It is important to be emotionally 'clean' in our work. Having worked on our own family of origin themes and dealing with emotional issues in personal therapy helps us as psychologists to achieve greater objectivity in the assessment and treatment of couples. There is no question that relationship counselling can potentially evoke strong counter-transference reactions and potentially distort our ability to be therapeutic.

I recommend Monica McGoldrick and Randy Gerson's (1985) comprehensive book *Genograms in Family Assessment*.

Reflect

Draw your own genogram and reflect upon family themes. When you consider your own family, think about interviewing the elders in your family. They may be the 'keepers' of the oral history and help you to understand themes and patterns that have shaped the family over the generations.

Formulation

This important therapeutic task begins in the first session. What is wrong in the relationship of this couple? What relationship patterns have been established from childhood? Why are they coming to see me now? Such dimensions of understanding come under 'case formulation'.

The data will include such information as initial impressions, presenting problems, history of the difficulty, previous therapy and solutions attempted, changes sought by the couple, any recent stressors or life changes, full genogram, prognosis and expected length of treatment including an appropriate treatment plan. While there has been a bias against any diagnosis of individuals in marital and family therapy, it is important to be aware of any individual psychopathology that can affect the couple relationship as well as the individuals. It is also important to understand couple issues such as deficits in communication, conflict resolution skills, emotional contracts, interlocking cognitive distortions and inappropriate or blocked emotions (Weeks & Treat, 1992, pp. 10–18). The ability to 'read' the couple's relationship and understand it in terms of dynamic patterns will increase with experience. I also think it is helpful to use the idea of collaborative case formulation from CBT in this area, as it also encourages the couple to take more responsibility for progress in therapy (Grant, Townend, Mills, & Cockx, 2009, p. 136).

There is a useful online assessment tool for couples on the Relate Institute website. This questionnaire leads to a computer generated report. Over 125,000 couples have done the questionnaire.

In this chapter I have considered the first interview and begun the process of assessment using the genogram. The next chapter will focus on beginning to understand how conflict will present in treatment, what characterises couple distress, and how this indicates what kind of support and interventions are most likely to be effective.

Chapter 4

The assessment of the relationship, including conflict

Dear Bruce,

I thought I'd drop you a line to thank you so much for your help in sorting through my problems recently. The difference in the atmosphere in our house is amazing ...

The most important lesson was that it is OK to argue! When you first told me to list the good things that can come from arguments, I thought you were joking and didn't answer, but later on when you mentioned some of the benefits of arguments I was quite stunned. I had thought that disputes were evil and to be avoided and had felt a failure because we had so many heated discussions. What a revelation it was to me to realise that all the fighting we'd done had in fact been constructive...

Regards, Nancy

(Extract from a letter from a patient.)

Criteria of assessment

In the first session the psychologist considers: 'What is wrong? Why is this relationship not working? Where is the pain?' Such questions are basic to assessment. Naturally, assessment continues through the process of treatment, but it is important at the beginning to gain a sense of direction and to develop a plan for treatment.

In this area there are various criteria for assessment. One obvious indicator is the developmental stage of the relationship: engaged, newlywed, first baby, young children, adolescent children, 'empty nest', retirement, frail aged or dependent care. Other criteria may include: presenting symptoms, degree of cohesion, communication, sense of reality, affect, boundaries, attitudes, or whatever seems important. Clifford Sager (1981) outlined a system of assessment based on contracts. He specified the following determinants: dependence, passivity, distance, abuse of power, dominance or submission, fear of abandonment, need to possess or control, level of anxiety, mechanisms of defence, understanding of love, gender identity, sexual expectations, cognitive style, and self acceptance. These are all useful and at some level should be taken into account. However, the reality of couple treatment is that many issues are presented as important. How do we distinguish between what is urgent, even important, and what has the highest priority?

In 2003, Australian social worker and academic Paul Gibney wrote *The Pragmatics of Therapeutic Practice*. He encouraged a process of assessment with sensitivity to the larger systemic issues. If there is a problem such as panic disorder then assessment will be assisted by getting a history of troubling symptoms. Gibney recommended questions like: 'When did it begin? What are the symptoms that trouble you the most? In what way has the problem changed?' In a context of relationship or family: 'Who noticed the problem first? Who is most affected by the problem?' Gibney summarised the need for a larger perspective: 'The assessment should include a clear description of the presenting problem, co-existing problems, historical and family contexts, the strengths and support networks of the patient, his or her experiences of their best achievements, happiest times, and most disorganised and dysfunctional episodes. Some ideas of what the patient expects and hopes to achieve in therapy and in what time frame would be helpful' (Gibney, 2003, p. 47). The big picture is important, but what has the highest priority?

I find it helpful to focus on the nature of conflict: 'What is the process? How healthy or unhealthy?' (especially noting the presence or absence of Gottman and Silver's [1999] 'four horsemen of the apocalypse'). This approach opens therapy to a considerable research base. I will suggest assessing the nature of conflict and using this to guide therapeutic interventions. I should also add that this chapter should be considered more an external perspective (phenomenological); the internal dynamic of the couple's emotional processes is equally important and considered more fully using EFT-C for couples in the next chapter.

Introducing the four stage approach

Conflict is inevitable in every intimate relationship. Some couples express it openly; whereas others attempt to deny it and express it indirectly. An example of a covert expression of conflict is passive–aggressive behaviour — *after an argument, Betty 'forgot' to pick up her husband from work.* It is usually helpful to normalise conflict because for some people it can be quite frightening.

Reflect

How do you handle conflict?

Think about the last significant relationship dispute in which you were involved. Did you or your partner:

- Raise your voices? Shout? Make comments about the character of your partner?
- Give personal insults or label?
- Were there any physical actions such as slamming doors, throwing things or violence?
- Did you resolve the dispute or just go around in circles?
- Did you involve anyone else such as children, in-laws or friends?
- Did anyone make threats?
- What followed the fight? Silence for a number of days? A passionate reconciliation?

It is helpful to consider the role of anger in the relationship. Anger can be used to protect an individual from feelings that are more difficult or painful such as shame, guilt, sadness, depression, powerlessness, mistrust and very commonly dependency. An underlying emotion might be fear. Consider the following scenario:

> Brett wanted comfort in his family when he was a child, but every time he got close to his mother she rejected him. So when he got close to Annie he found himself getting very angry because he feared the possibility of rejection.

With anger there is always hurt, and this is a better focus because it is more inviting for the partner. EFT-C distinguishes between primary and secondary emotions, and will be further explained in the next chapter.

Anger may have specific functions in the relationship. It is a common way of regulating intimacy — or distance. It can be used to test the commitment of the partner to the relationship:

> If Harry keeps coming back after I have thrown him out of the house then I know I can depend upon him.

Anger can be used to dominate and exercise power in a relationship. Violent people commonly use anger in this way. Anger can serve positive functions as well such as a response to the violation of a boundary of the self or the relationship. The discovery of an affair is such a betrayal and the injured party is usually very angry. So anger is a given. Even reciprocal anger is quite natural. In itself it is not dysfunctional; however, it can be badly mishandled in a relationship leading to hurtful and damaging exchanges.

Exercise

One helpful way to understand anger in the family is to do a genogram following the theme of anger in the family with the following questions:

- How did your parents deal with anger or conflict?
- How did you see them work through it?

- Who got angry in your family, and how did the others respond?
- What did you learn about anger from both parents?
- When a parent was angry with you, what did you feel? What did you do?
- When you got angry, who listened or failed to listen to you?
- How did members of your family respond when you got angry?
- Who was allowed and not allowed to be angry in the family?
- Was anyone ever seriously hurt when someone got angry? (Weeks & Treat, 1992, pp. 140–141).

Issues of conflict generally are the focus of counselling sessions and foundational to learning how to have better skills in working on points of disagreement. Guerin, Fay, Burden, and Kautto (1987) suggested a four-stage model for evaluating and treating marital conflict, which works with a range of couples and presenting difficulties.

STAGE I

This stage is usually found during courtship, or for those who have recently entered a de facto relationship, or in the first years of marriage. Generally there is a low level of conflict. All the signs of a healthy relationship are present: communication is open, polarisation of power is minimal, the individuals are generally self-focused (with only occasional bursts of projection), the level of reactivity and criticism is low, and trust is still secure. It is the 'cocoon' stage and will not last forever!

> Thomas is a 50-year-old divorcee who is planning to get married. Maggie is 37 years old and has not been married before. They have known each other for five years, but only in the last few months has the relationship become intimate. The date for marriage has been set. They came into counselling because of conflict between Maggie and Tom's two teenage children. The couple are beginning to see that a blended family is more complicated than they had thought.

STAGE II

There is more turbulence in this stage. Conflict can be intense. The picture is mixed: communication is reasonably open, but criticism and reactivity have increased; there is a more restricted expression of personal thought and feelings; projection is more prevalent, and the couple will experience conflict as less safe. However, credibility is still high. There is a power struggle in the relationship, which may be marked by a 'win or lose' mentality, but it is more playful than desperate. The progression from expectation to alienation has now reached hurt and anger with a residue of resentment. Goodwill remains, but it is under threat.

> Claire and Bill have been married for four years. Both have been reasonably happy in the marriage. They have come to see a psychologist because of a crisis. The problem is that Bill had too many drinks at the office Christmas party and he slept with a colleague. Claire has been obsessed about the incident. Bill can't understand what happened and is quick to assure Claire that it will not be repeated.

After the honeymoon of Stage I is over, hard work and intense negotiation begins. Hopefully, this will establish a better working relationship blending the skills, needs and style of interaction of both in the couple relationship. Often the emotional high of early attraction has faded and one or both will begin to doubt if they are still 'in love' with the other.

STAGE III

The stress in the relationship is now very high. The emotional climate may be marked by extremes of 'hot and cold'. Reactivity may be sudden and sharp. The power struggle is now deadly — as if personal survival depends upon winning. There may be a limited capacity even to exchange information, either personal or general. What may be labelled 'self-disclosure' is often no more than a dumping of accumulated emotions, and is inevitably heard as criticism or complaint. Credibility is now fading. Self-focus is fleeting and projection is the usual means of interaction. Bitterness has accumulated. It is usual for at least one of the couple to have withdrawn into numbness and detachment.

The conflict in this stage is characterised by high emotional arousal, polarised positions of fixed distance, and rigid blame of the spouse. The relationship is stuck in mutual pain. A sense of despair may be felt acutely by one of the partners. The possibility of separation is now an open issue. The relationship is clearly in trouble.

> Don and Tanya have been married 15 years. Over this period there has been occasional violence and Tanya has had a number of affairs. Money has been a topic of dispute for nearly all of the marriage. Their children tend to take sides and join in the family 'uproar'. Don has recently become a counsellor at Lifeline and wants to work on improving the marriage.

While Geurin et al. (1987) have some criteria for assessing conflict in Stage III, I think it is best to think about how trust in the relationship has deteriorated. There is also a dominance of destructive patterns in dealing with conflict. In couples where there is domestic violence it is imperative to assess the risk factors for members of the family, and if you consider the risk to be serious to intervene, if necessary, to keep people safe.

Stage III Checklist

1. Unresolved issues have been the focus of conflict for more than six months.

2. Cycles of conflict are out of control. The couple sometimes fight in front of close friends or relatives. At times there is emotional chaos.

3. Generally there are complications such as an affair or affairs, incidents of violence, or problems with an addiction.

4. There are problems with jealousy or trust.

5. There are concerns that one of the couple has withdrawn emotional attachment or may have given up.

6. It is common that one, or perhaps both, believe that the partner has a problem in their character and if this was 'fixed up' most of the pressure would be taken off the relationship.

7. There is resentment about past behaviour.

8. The possibility of separation or divorce has been discussed.

All of these items are typical of this stage.

STAGE IV

The end of the marriage is now in sight. Guerin et al. (1987) marked this stage by the decision of one or both to engage the services of a lawyer. This is not always the 'point of no return', but it usually places the couple in an adversarial context. There is usually a mood of resignation with the individual who has sought legal advice.

> Angus and Sue have been separated for eight months. They are having intense conflict about the property settlement and visitation arrangements. David's lawyer suggested that they see a mediator to try to work out current problems.

I would add another indicator: the 'trial separation'. In this case counselling can assist the process in helping the couple to structure their separation, decide how often and where to meet each other, or communicate by phone or email. It is a time in which both will need to be getting support from friends and family members rather than from each other or the children. Having romantic contact with others is best discussed so that trust is not further undermined. My co-author Malise tells people that they may never take up this option in the trial separation, but it is good to have an agreement about it. The leaver may already be seeing someone else and may be glad to have this in the open. Sometimes it is a sobering experience and may lead to a new willingness to work on the relationship. If not, then they are one step ahead in forming new networks and connections. It is appropriate to warn about the danger of rebound relationships, but encourage the expansion of social networks.

It is not always easy for a psychologist to know whether the relationship is beyond reconciliation. Some couples enter counselling with a surface willingness to work on issues but one partner may have an agenda of separation. Sometimes self-justification is the reason: 'I did everything I could'. A person may want to leave a dependent, poorly functioning partner in the care of the treating psychologist. Since it takes two to make a relationship work, both need to be willing to participate in the therapeutic process. The reality is that either can 'pull the plug' and then the counselling enters the separation mode.

It can be useful to point out that if the couple has children, it will take improved communication to co-parent as separated parents. And a better understanding of themselves as individuals, as well as what went wrong, will help to avoid some of the pitfalls in future relationships.

Appropriate interventions
One advantage of the four-stage model of relationship conflict is that it broadly suggests what kinds of intervention are most likely to be effective.

STAGE I
In the 'honeymoon' period of the relationship the couple have accumulated little emotional baggage and there is an abundance of motivation, open communication, trust, and low anxiety. Difficulties can usually be met with an educational approach. The couple can generally use information in a functional way, rather than getting caught up in dysfunctional patterns.

Most marriage preparation courses are based on such an approach and generally this is appropriate given the developmental stage of the couple. I was once involved in a church-run course that 'graduated' over a hundred couples per year, developed by Bishop Ian George (then Archdeacon) at St Johns Anglican Church, Reid in Canberra in the 1980s. The topics included marital expectations, values, fears, conflict resolution, legal and financial matters, sexuality and birth control, and a rehearsal of the wedding ceremony. Although there is a lot of value in these courses, there is an inherent dilemma that the couples most motivated to come will need it less than more avoidant couples. The latter are harder to reach through adult education courses and are less likely to seek help when the relationship is in trouble.

An example of what might be taught are the 'fair fight rules' of Mace (1948):

• Know what you are fighting about.

• Stick to the topic.

• Don't attack the other person (e.g., call them names).

• Time your fight as carefully as possible.

• Keep quarrels private.

This kind of guide sometimes helps couples to realise that conflict is natural and can potentially contribute to the growth of a relationship. An analogy of 'weeding a garden' can be helpful. An educational and problem-solving approach was also recommended by Montgomery and Evans (1989), both Australian clinical psychologists.

I would also recommend family-of-origin work and teaching strategies for handling conflict in a respectful way. You can ask the couple to read relevant books and to try to do suggested exercises. The major drawback is that an educational approach tends to fail with more intense or ingrained conflict.

Australian clinical psychologist Kim Halford has been a leader in the education of couples for more satisfying relationships. A good review of this research is the article 'Best practice in couple relationship education' (Halford, Markman, Kling, & Stanley, 2007). Halford, with his team, has developed a very useful resource — *Couple Care*, which includes DVDs and six units focusing on self-change. There is also a targeted program — *Couple Care for Parents*.

STAGE II

A couple will usually wait until they feel stuck and out of control before seeking help for their relationship. This is true for Stage II as well as the later stages. It is useful to validate the pain that both are feeling. Yes, there may be problems that require help from a psychologist, but this does not mean that the relationship is over. Such a reassurance based on an accurate assessment can be a source of relief.

In this stage, Geurin et al. (1987) recommends that the conflict can be directly addressed. Since problems are not so chronic or complex, progress can be made by directly addressing the issues.

> Dan and Joan sought help because an emotional pattern of pursuit and distance was causing frustrating difficulties. Dan worked long hours as a junior partner in an accountancy firm. Joan understood the need for establishing his role in the company, but complained when he took on the voluntary job of treasurer at a local football club. The psychologist coached Joan to experiment with being more distant and paying attention to her feelings. After a few weeks Joan discovered that she pursued as a means of soothing inner anxiety. Dan was initially delighted with the extra space, but then found that he was getting angry. He used his time alone as a way to calm down, but found to his surprise that he needed Joan to take the initiative for emotional contact, even in the form of 'nagging'.

It is important to help the couple change their perspective. When a marriage is in difficulties, each person tends to become an expert on the behaviour of their partner and project blame in the process. The therapeutic process tries to reverse this and to enhance self-focus.

> Joan soon began to find other ways to meet her needs. She joined a Chinese cooking class and saw some high school friends for coffee. She reasoned that she was a social person and needed more emotional support than was available in the marriage. Joan also pointed out that she was acting for herself and not against Dan. Gradually they realised that they had a common problem in both wanting and fearing intimacy. The way was clear to explore ways to find a better balance.

Couples also tend to confuse closeness with sameness (i.e., understanding each other's point of view with agreement). However, it is almost axiomatic that 'opposites attract'. Such initial differences can add spice to the relationship, but later may become irritating. So commonly couples will invest enormous energy in the 'blaming game'. This involves looking for 'who started it'. The search for the beginning of the sequence is futile, as it is usually more of a circular dance: 'the behaviour of one partner maintains and provokes the other' (Lerner, 1985, p. 56). In the previous case example, Joan used her pain as a stimulus for personal change, which soon led to changes in the relationship.

The treating psychologist can help the couple to see the cost of unresolved and badly handled relationship conflict: emotional distancing, numbness and the possible death of feelings, destructive triangles, game playing, bitterness, self-fulfilling prophesies, and employing the children in family warfare. Couples in difficulties will usually have poor conflict resolution strategies, which provide an important target for intervention.

Gottman (1999) observed that couples rarely relate to each other with active listening. Once negative emotions enter, everyone responds in kind — even in happy marriages! Ultimately happiness in a relationship is more about the process of conflict rather than an ideal of 'good communication'. Gottman found 'the four horsemen of the apocalypse' that predict relationship failure:

1. **Criticism.** There will always be complaints in a relationship but criticism is personal: 'You always …, you never …'. And the range of 'why' questions that aren't really questions at all (more insults actually). It is an attack on the personality or character of the partner.

2. **Contempt.** This conveys an ugliness in a relationship and is associated with cynicism, sarcasm, eye-rolling, hostile humour, and mockery. The contemptuous person assumes the 'higher ground'. It is pure poison in a relationship and virtually absent in happy relationships.

3. **Defensiveness.** While this can be understandable, it is blaming — 'you are the problem' — and rarely helps because the partner may 'turn up the heat' in order to be 'heard'.

4. **Stonewalling.** This involves tuning out or not hearing the partner. It is a protection against feeling flooded.

It is essential to help the couple begin to identify such relationship patterns and then begin to change towards healthier styles of interaction. This is a priority of treatment with all the stages, but in later stages it will be more difficult.

I find the distinction of complaint and criticism can be very helpful and take some of the 'sting' out of conflict. The couple will often squabble and you have material on which to focus and coach them in expressing their points in a constructive way. It is also important to affirm Gottman's axiom: 'Most marital arguments cannot be resolved'. Most couples spend years trying to change the other's mind or way of seeing an issue (Gottman & Silver, 1999, p. 23). It is better to understand the bottom line of what is hard to change and learn how to live with difference by honouring and respecting each other. Only then can the couple build a shared sense of meaning and purpose.

Gottman (1999, p. 193) talked about finding an antidote to each of the destructive patterns. With defensiveness the answer is to accept responsibility for part of the problem. Contempt is best met by creating a culture of praise and pride in the other. And stonewalling is best met by self-soothing, giving feedback through listening and staying emotionally connected. Many of the standard skills taught in clinical psychology programs are useful at this point — for example, breathing, countering negative and catastrophic thinking, visualisation of a safe place, noticing areas of tension in the body and stress reduction strategies. Biofeedback may also be used.

The best time to learn emotional skills is while an emotion is hot. When better to learn to contain anger than when feeling intense rage in a session? It is in the emotional 'hot house' that the best learning is possible and can be encouraged by the treating psychologist (see Gottman, 1999, p. 180–181). The couple can learn new skills which can be built upon with 'scaffolding' (Vygotsky, 1962). Gottman (1999) asked how to make relationship therapy a positive experience

> ... to help partners to find a way to honour both of their life dreams, which underlie their most gridlocked conflicts ... the entire problem-solving process is recast as one of identifying and harmonising people's basic life dreams ... it can even have that self-indulgent quality that is so wonderfully attractive about individual therapy' (p. 184.)

A genogram can lead to insight:

> Dan admitted problems with trusting Joan. This was connected with his father's addiction to gambling. He grew up with the unspoken rule 'Don't trust', which was part of survival in an environment of broken promises. All along Joan had been blaming herself: 'What have I done wrong?' It suddenly made a lot of sense!

Couples in this stage can benefit from insight. It helps to see what they have experienced as frustrating in a larger context and to use their mutual regard in productive ways.

I also encourage couples to build their friendship. To simply solve all points of conflict would leave a void. It is an obvious but important point that couples who stay in a relationship and are happy like each other! Gottman and Silver (1999, p. 19) said that 'happy marriages are based on a deep friendship'. This protects against the negative emotions that can easily overwhelm a relationship. Positive feelings are pervasive, so after an ambiguous exchange one does not jump to a negative conclusion: *Bill is putting me down*. It is a worthwhile goal to try to set the relationship at a positive level.

A good indicator of the health of a relationship is the level of 'goodwill'. To what degree is there respect and expressions of care for the other person? A husband in Stage II said of his wife: 'I really love Anne and I want our marriage to work, but there are a few things that drive me crazy!'. Both are more willing to work on the problem once it is clearly identified. Another strength of couples in this stage is that they can still say: 'I am sorry'. Attempts at repair are more successful and less likely to be rebuffed by the partner. This helps in lowering emotional reactivity and changing dysfunctional patterns.

STAGE III

It is important to distinguish this stage of conflict from the previous two stages. Guerin et al. (1987, p. 150) warn that if the psychologist moves to focus on issues the result may be to create further confusion. More groundwork may be necessary.

It may be hard to predict exactly how the couple will present in the sessions. There is intense emotional reactivity. This is characteristic of intense fusion, with the reaction of 'distance, the two ping-pong back and forth between fusion and distance. Over time, the emotional climate tends to deteriorate' (Fogarty, 1976, pp. 144–153). The couple may appear to have lost control over the cycles of conflict. This is, of course, highly damaging to the relationship: it erodes caring, rubs salt in emotional wounds, and diminishes self-esteem.

One aspect of process that can be addressed is what Gottman (1999) calls a 'harsh start-up' to marital conflict. Generally by Stage III there is such pent-up frustration in the relationship that anger flares and negative emotions readily surface — usually explosively! This is usually associated with storing up grievances in the relationship. The treating psychologist can draw attention to how conflict begins and encourage the couple to raise concerns more gently. He noted that women are more likely to initiate conflict by making a demand and then to criticise, men are more likely to stonewall. Both are highly connected with relationship distress and ultimately its failure (p. 41).

I think it also important to understand the 'principle of relationship influence'. The problem with being defensive or stonewalling is that it is inherently rejecting of all that a partner might say or do. Rather than rebuff, the spouse recognises the value of what his or her partner might offer by way of a different perspective. There is a helpful listening to the partner, understanding the issues seen by the other, and trying to find options that bring together mutual concerns about an issue.

Defensiveness can lead to stonewalling. It is not surprising that a person will seek to repress feelings. This is a system of containment, a kind of 'filing' of emotions away, and the result is the loss of awareness that the pain ever existed: 'This phenomenon contributes to the myth that stonewallers don't have feelings, they are cold and emotionless' (Guerin et al., 1987, p. 191). Under pressure, this defence can break down and emotions flow in every direction. This can be very frightening since it is a loss of emotional control. I have also found that there may be a risk that the container, usually the male, might become briefly suicidal.

The initial task for the psychologist is to restore order. Structure reduces anxiety. Do not allow the couple to interrupt each other or make personal attacks. If this is impossible then it may be wise to see them separately for a few sessions. If a decision has to be made it might be best to keep the focus on the process. For example:

> *Husband:* 'She thinks I lie!'
>
> *Psychologist:* 'Then trust is an issue. How do we work out a way for the school fees to be paid? Would you like to brainstorm for say 10 minutes?'
>
> And later.
>
> *Psychologist:* 'So you believe John when he tells you that he has had a promotion, but not when he tells you who he has had lunch with. What criteria do you use for when to believe what he has said?'

This also helps the couple to begin to think rather than simply react. It is too simplistic to assume that venting feelings will clear the air — it may further confuse matters. More often than not displays of anger are part of the relationship dance. In fact, the ventilating of anger can give a false feeling of being in charge (Jansen, 1989, p. 167). Alternatively, if the other partner has had trouble expressing anger then it may be helpful to encourage that individual to express feelings, even at the risk of heightening conflict. This will help to end the myth that one spouse has a monopoly on any one emotion in the relationship.

It is natural under stress to blame the other, but this is not likely to lead to significant change. A treatment goal is to enhance self-focus, which reduces the natural tendency to blame the partner and introduces healthy change into the relationship. The basic rule is that self-focus reduces reactivity.

It is also helpful to guide the couple in managing physiological arousal. If either is feeling flooded, then the old wisdom of taking a break is very justified. Gottman (1999, p. 82) recommended a minimum of 20 minutes, followed by re-engaging on the issue.

A review of current stresses has the effect of broadening what may be a limited perspective.

> Jack and Carrie were aware of difficulties in their capacity to resolve arguments, but they did not appreciate the effect of accumulated pressure from the loss of Jack's job, the deteriorating health of Carrie's mother, their youngest child's falling grades, and financial problems.

The larger context also helps to address what might be a secret fear that they are failing in their marriage because they are bad people (Jansen, 1989, p. 217).

While EFT-C will be more closely examined in the following chapters, it is relevant to dealing with difficult couples in Stage III. Think about helping to reduce volatility with emotional regulation strategies: mindfulness, progressive muscle relaxation (PMR), breathing, safe place visualisations, and so on. This may need to be done in individual sessions as well. It is also helpful to use key concepts of EFT-C to better understand and work with emotional processes, but at this stage moving between some focus on issues of conflict and additional structural support is important.

Bitterness is usually present in Stage III. Guerin et al. (1987) used the metaphor of making deposits in a 'bitter bank' and collecting interest. This metaphor is self-focusing and may help an individual gain awareness of the real cost of making such deposits. The psychologist can help to trace bitterness back to early expectations in the relationship. This may provide opportunities for comparison with prior family experiences. A longitudinal perspective can help.

> Psychologist: 'You were disappointed when Jack didn't notice your extra efforts in cooking. Were those feelings familiar?'
>
> Carrie: 'Yes, once I brought home a report card. Every grade was improved, but Dad only grunted'.

This links present feelings to past experiences. It also helps to contradict such myths as: 'I was happy until I met Jack'. The genogram may reveal bitterness as a family pattern. Jack can see that men in his family typically have negative images of women; Carrie can see a long history of women as passive martyrs. The genogram can also be used to identify family-of-origin triggers for conflict, conscious and unconscious contracts, role expectations, family rules, classic double binds, jealousy (usually linked to excessive dependency), and 'crazy-making situations'. It is also helpful, using EFT-C, to distinguish primary and secondary emotions, but more about this in the next chapter.

Although I have described this stage in terms of turbulent emotions, this is not always the case. There may be icy hostility or emotional deadness with almost nothing said. The mood may be quiet and despairing — like being at a funeral when death was unexpected. But whatever the mood, progress in this stage is usually slow and difficult.

A final thought about Stage III. One partner may have a fantasy solution. This is an idealised answer to the problems. Such a 'solution' may be divorce, living alone, an affair, or death of the spouse. This may provide the content of daydreams. Unfortunately, this person will move away from working on the relationship towards the dream. If this is a problem, which may be sensed in lack of commitment to the counselling process, it may be necessary to have this possibility brought into the open and 'reality tested', possibly in an individual session. The psychologist can then more realistically point out that separation is always an option but hardly a solution.

Some relationships are remarkably stable in spite of intense and turbulent conflict. It is one way of binding anxiety and there are some positive aspects:

- Conflict can provide a sense of emotional contact with the other person.

- The tension and arguments justify both partners maintaining a comfortable emotional distance without feeling guilty.

- It is easy to project blame onto the other and then feel in control, as well as self-justified.

- As it absorbs anxiety, Kerr (1988, p. 193) pointed out: 'So spouses in a conflictual marriage are less vulnerable to physical, emotional, or social symptoms. In addition, children of conflict-filled marriages are less vulnerable to symptoms'.

This stage is quite a challenge to the psychologist. I find it helpful to think in terms of what Australian social worker Michael White calls 'unique outcomes' (White & Epston, 1990). From session to session we can notice progress by underlining the differences in the evolving relationship. Often the couple hardly seems to notice, but identifying the change is very encouraging.

Often it helps to mention that in a relationship we have little power to change our partner, but we can change ourselves and open the way for possible change in the relationship. For example, a defensive spouse may surprise the critical partner by not defending himself, but agreeing with the criticism. This is likely to de-escalate the usual barrage of accusations and leave space for a different conversation to occur.

It is commitment that makes all the difference. Not a commitment to romantic bliss, but to the partner in a realistic sense:

> Commitment means that one will not make a silent judgment and withdraw, wishing the 'loved' person dead, but that one will risk conflict, again and again, to achieve the pleasure of mutual attentiveness ... the acceptance of the ordeal by conflict is caring (Shapiro, 1984, p. 59).

In addition to commitment, the most important factor is self-focus. I am reminded of the words of Jesus:

> Why do you see the speck in your brother's eye, but do not notice the log in your own eye ... first take the log out of your own eye, and then you will see clearly to take the speck out of your brother's eye (Matthew 7:3,5).

Such wisdom is timeless.

STAGE IV

Theologian Paul Tillich once described reality as that which we have to adapt to since it will not adjust to us. This is certainly true in the breakdown of a relationship or marriage. It is not any particular emotion that dominates, though anger and bitterness are certainly common. The sad reality is that 'Marriages, like people, most often die as they have lived' (Guerin et al., 1987, p. 249). Pain is the only constant. As Virginia Satir once observed about the hurt of rejection, there are two messages heard by the individual: 'No!' and 'You're no damn good!'

The end is usually resisted by one partner, but even that person's motivation to change will not be enough to save the marriage. The only glimmer of hope is when the partner who has initiated legal action has some ambivalence. In this case the psychologist can:

- help each spouse to determine his or her 'bottom line'
- define what options remain other than separation or divorce

- encourage both partners to understand more fully in what ways they contributed to the failure of the relationship.

The importance of drawing a bottom line is obvious. Usually it is psychologically necessary for the reluctant partner to be able to let the relationship go, for Alice to say to herself: 'I can live without being with Jason'. Only then can she say: 'These are the things I cannot or will not tolerate in the marriage'. Ideally, it is not a reactive position. It is then possible to assure the spouse that this position is acting for the self and not against them. A bottom-line position evolves naturally from self-focus. What is my attitude to my partner's drinking? Toleration of affairs? Verbal violence? It is also necessary in the process of separation. What access do I want? What property settlement? Will I take this to court? There is no right solution for all people. Rather, the bottom-line position should derive from an individual's self-respect, values, integrity, and dignity.

Another approach to counselling at this stage is to help draw up a contract of 'structured separation' as recommended by Donald Granvold (1983). The couple negotiate a written contract specifying expected behaviour in the following areas: commitment to ongoing counselling, duration of separation, frequency of contact between partners, sexual intimacy between them, dating, sexual contact with others, privacy, and access to children. This structure is helpful in such an uncertain time because it is so objective and concrete. Granvold later added the following items to a separation contract: no final decision until the end of the agreed period, financial support, homework during counselling, and re-negotiation (pp. 404–408). This has the intention of allowing decisions to be made about the future of the relationship in an ordered and, hopefully, more secure way.

When is it time to tell the children about a separation? Perhaps it is best done when the parents have made concrete plans. They should not try to 'tell it all'. Glenda Banks gave as a general rule: 'Don't bite off more than your child can swallow' (Banks, 1981,

p. 23). It is helpful to stress that the children were not responsible for the separation, and that both parents will continue to love and care for them. Unfortunately, in this tense time it is easy for the children to become victims of displaced rage. Other inappropriate behaviours include attempts to win children as allies, quizzing for information about the ex-partner, and asking them to be 'adult' confidants. Sometimes it is important to help the separating couple to distinguish marital problems from parental responsibilities.

It is generally acknowledged that children adjust better with both parents having free access. However, there may be factors that affect the welfare of the children, such as mental illness, alcoholism, violence and sexual abuse. In addition court custody battles exact an emotional cost from all involved.[2] In this difficult period one role of the psychologist is to help with 'damage control'. Chapter 10 of this book provides information about the effect of divorce on children and how to manage this phase in the most healthy way possible. It may be helpful for people to read books such as *Shared Care or Divided Lives* (Watts, 2008), and to be given handouts about the needs of children at various ages from Kalter (1990).

In spite of all the difficulties, the extended family should not be neglected. The psychologist can encourage children to visit grandparents (who may worry about ever seeing them again), aunts, uncles, cousins, and family friends. This may also open up other avenues of support. There may also be support from community or church groups.

The reluctant spouse may feel considerable anxiety about the future. Reassuring messages can help: 'What you are going through is normal; I have every confidence that you will survive and make another life for yourself. You are not going crazy'. If distress is very high, it may be necessary to assist your patient sort out priorities, list daily responsibilities, verbalise fears and rehearse new behaviours. If the person remains unrealistic in still chasing the spouse, then some form of confrontation about 'letting go' will be necessary. There is some excellent material on the emotional journey of grief after the end of a relationship and this can be offered.

The emotionally contained person will generally present as more calm. There is a risk, however, that they will move too fast out of the relationship. This can mean going to live with the 'other person' or moving out of town. Sometimes this is an attempt to cover feelings of loss. It is also possible that 'they are running faster in response to their spouse's desperate behaviour, afraid that they might look back at their own ambivalence and change their minds' (Guerin et al., 1987, p. 251).

The legal system is best left to the guidance of lawyers specialising in family law. However, there are often difficulties that can spill over into counselling because the relationship has been placed in an adversarial context. Lawyers may well have goals such as getting the best deal for their client or winning sole custody. These goals may be counter to therapeutic aims and a wise balance is needed, especially when you want to work towards cooperative parenting. In the past I have advised couples to look at services of mediation that attempt to help them work out their own settlement, with the proviso that legal representatives of both parties should check over any written agreement. There are also some hopeful signs that the largely adversarial system might have alternatives, and some lawyers are trying different approaches with more of a client rather than conflict focus.

Counselling in this stage is often with only one person, the other having left or having no desire to work on the relationship. The Bowen style of therapy is not limited by access to only one person. Introducing change through the more motivated individual can reverberate throughout a family system. It is common for the focus to shift gradually from the ex-partner to the self. This enables the taking of responsibility and moving towards a different future. Naturally it is best to work on increasing strengths rather than shoring up weaknesses.

The present high divorce rate is not because marriage is less important, but because relationships have become all important. Also there seems to be greater demands from society, with fewer supports. Expectations easily escalate and an individual can have little tolerance for the imperfect partner or a less than ideal lifestyle. It is sad that couples ask so much from each other and appear so unwilling to give in return.

Is separation a failure? Sometimes yes and sometimes no. It is a therapeutic success when a person can take responsibility for past actions, learn from experience, have insights into what went wrong, gain some awareness of emotional patterns from the original family, and be willing to trust their real self in a new relationship.

In this chapter an external perspective on couple conflict has been presented, conceptualised by Geurin's four stages, and drawing on Gottman's research. Equally important is the understanding of emotional processes in relationship distress. This will be more fully addressed in the next chapter using EFT-C. What exactly constitutes a happy marriage is also relevant (Halford, Kelly, & Markman, 1997).

Chapter 5

Emotional processes underlying relationship conflict

What is most fundamental? The answer is easy: emotions. They are the building blocks of a relationship. It has been noted: 'Emotion binds couples together, but it is also what rips them apart' (Greenberg & Goldman, 2008, p. 20). No couple therapist will go too far astray following the 'hot spots' of emotional processing in working with couples. It always *feels* relevant.

Emotion-focused therapy (EFT-C), with a sophisticated developmental and personality theory, is practical in application and has a growing body of evidence for its effectiveness (an evidence-based therapy [EBT]). In this chapter, I will outline the place of emotions and briefly give some guidelines for therapeutic interventions. I recommend any clinical psychologist interested in practising EFT-C to read widely, attend courses offered by training institutes and get supervision from an experienced practitioner. In Australia, start with the Institute for Emotionally Focused Therapy in Sydney (see www.eftherapy.com).

The goal for both therapist and couple is a mutual understanding and the challenge to learn a set of skills. But it is like putting up a tent. The difficulty is not the mechanics or the 'how to', but dealing with the emotional intensity of relationships. It is a tent put up in gale force winds. Consider the following case example of William and Betty.

> The first thing I noticed about Bill was his 'old school tie', which did not match in colour the rest of his clothes. His wife Betty followed him into my office. She strode with determination.

They were both in their late fifties.

Bill explained the problem: 'I've been offered a temporary promotion to our branch office in Rome. It's a wonderful opportunity, which I will not see again before I retire. It's for only nine months ...'

Betty interrupted: 'But he'll be leaving me behind for that time! It's just like when he works late and goes on all those trips interstate. I never see him.'

Psychologist to Betty: 'I would imagine that is frustrating?'

Betty: 'I have given up on expecting him to care. I raised the children is this is the "thanks" I get!'

Psychologist: 'You are angry about how he has treated you? But maybe also you feel neglected and lonely.'

Betty nods and is unable to speak.

When we explored more of the reason for Bill wanting to take the overseas position and how exciting he thought living briefly in Italy might be, he continued:

Bill: 'I just feel overwhelmed, almost smothered by Betty's demands. She is constantly negative and criticising, when I am lucky (with sarcasm), mostly it is blame and barely contained rage.'

Psychologist: 'You feel overwhelmed. It is just too much.'

Bill said quietly: 'I have been thinking about leaving. I know it's a big step after 30 years of marriage but I thought that I could use the months in Rome as a trial to see how I got on alone.'

Betty: 'So that's why you want to leave me behind? It's not just the inadequate living allowance? You bastard! I suspected as much!'

It was obvious that Bill and Betty had an imbalance in their pattern of distancing and pursuing, but the underlying emotional turmoil was also clear and it had led to mutual pain, resentment and even despair. I had an individual session with Bill and he was able to express his anger over what he considered were excessive demands and no recognition of the effort he had made to be a 'good provider'. I needed a few sessions with

Betty alone for her to acknowledge her level of dependence in the relationship and to see that her anger was pushing Bill away — now and perhaps through the years of their marriage. The prospect of the end of the marriage was very frightening to her: 'How will I be able to manage? The children are grown up. Who would want me?'

Motivation

We might consider Bill and Betty's emotional investments in terms of EFT-C's three motivators:

1. *Attachment and connection.* Susan Johnson has written extensively on the importance of attachment and how it is important in affect regulation (Johnson & Whiffen, 1999). This need was most obvious in Betty who was more pursuing and wanted emotional connection with her husband. Perhaps underlying emotions might include primitive fears of annihilation and abandonment.

2. *Identity influence.* Greenberg has articulated the importance of understanding emotional processes in the formation and maintenance of identity as well as working with issues of influence, power and control (Greenberg & Goldman, 2008). This appeared to be of central importance to Bill with the offer of a promotion in Rome and perhaps a boost to his self-esteem. It is natural that he would protect his identity and resist external attempts at definition. Associated negative emotions might include shame, fear, powerlessness and anger.

3. *Attraction and liking.* This recognises that positive feelings are generated when partners are interested in, like and feel attracted to each other. Naturally this is important for the maintenance of intimate bonds (Greenberg & Goldman, 2008, p. 6). It is a feeling for the other. Love clearly relates to attachment, but additionally involves behavioural systems such as caregiving and sexual expression (Greenberg & Goldman, 2008, p. 84). Perhaps both Bill and Betty might have difficulty recalling this but attraction was a factor that drew them

together and led to their happiness in the early years of their marriage. If the marriage is to survive it will be important, at some stage in the therapy, to find ways to resurrect such feelings for this couple so warmth, pleasure and happiness might return.

The EFT-C approach uses the treating psychologist as a coach for emotions and essentially to encourage the couple to identify and express their unexpressed adult needs. Another goal is to assist the couple to be more skilled at self-regulation, to observe and change dysfunctional patterns and to manage when the partner is not available to respond compassionately.

Understanding emotions

Emotions have been classified in various ways. Greenberg and Goldman (2008) identified the broadly negative: sadness, shyness, shame, guilt, fear and self-directed hostility. The more positive are surprise, enjoyment, and excitement. Contempt, anger and disgust toward others can be thought of as a 'hostile triad'. Of course we do not simply feel one thing at a time, rather there are many possibilities in interactions with others. More specifically:

> sadness and fear prototypically relate to attachment, security, and connection; joy and excitement prototypically relate to love, which appears to combine many emotions into a unique and mysterious blend; contempt, disgust and anger — the hostile triad — relate to dominance and threats to identity. (Greenberg & Goldman, 2008, p. 40).

It would be simplistic to assert that people are only motivated by affects, but clearly the emotional dimension is important and at times of central concern. EFT-C recognises the importance of affect regulation in dyadic relationships (Stern, 1985). The two important needs are for security and validation, which are present from birth to death, and both contribute in adulthood to the creation and maintenance of wellbeing. The couple therapist will need to focus on enhancing the ability of both to regulate their own affect and not turn their distress into attack or withdrawal; 'so a balance needs to be struck in all relationships between good-enough responsiveness and good-enough self-regulation' (Greenberg & Goldman, 2008, p. 45).

The ability to self-sooth gives some margin for not instantly reacting in stressful situations. Often there is too great a sense of entitlement in marital relationships: that the partner has to be there in exactly the right way, when and how needed. This is a source of great unhappiness. Instead 'marital harmony has to do with both (a) greater accessibility and responsiveness, and (b) greater ability to tolerate some disappointment, separation, criticisms, and disagreement and still respond non-defensively and compassionately to one's partner's needs' (Greenberg & Goldman, 2008, p. 47).

EFT-C makes a distinction between emotions that are adaptive and maladaptive in couple relationships. This includes:

- *Primary emotions* that are the person's most fundamental and original reaction to a situation. This includes sadness in relation to loss, anger in response to violation, and fear in response to threat. These emotions are attachment and identity-orientated, and they enhance the self and intimate bonds.

- *Secondary emotions* are the emotional reactions that are secondary to the primary and indeed may be defences. Examples include anger in response to being hurt, crying when angry, feeling afraid or guilty about being angry. It is not so much in response to a situation but to initial feelings. Secondary emotions, if too intense, need to be down-regulated and explored in order to get to the primary emotions that have not been expressed.

- *Instrumental emotions* are those expressed to influence others and to get them to respond in certain ways; for example, to cry 'crocodile tears' and get sympathy.

- *Maladaptive emotions* are the old familiar bad feelings that stem from past trauma, wounds from unmet childhood needs or unfinished business, say from a previous partner. Indeed these feelings 'leave people feeling stuck, overwhelmed, and out of control emotionally, and they generally need to be down-regulated and transformed' (Greenberg & Goldman, 2008, p. 51). Such emotional patterns lead to an experience of 'not me' states and are difficult to change.

EFT-C helps the couple to be more emotionally aware, especially of the softer primary emotions underlying attachment and identity needs. The awareness of what is driving negative cycles can lead to a more realistic choice to change patterns. There is also an appreciation of emotional style. Some people are overregulated or shut down in terms of emotional expression; whereas others are underregulated and overly expressive, especially of negative emotions. You can use CBT, dialectical behaviour therapy (DBT) and mindfulness techniques to assist in emotional regulation. This can also help the overregulated to be more emotionally aware. Greenberg also has some ideas about how to use emotions to transform dysfunctional emotions by a 'corrective emotional experience' (Greenberg & Goldman, 2008, pp. 56–57).

Cycles of emotional interaction

In EFT-C a reaction in a partner is not seen as 'caused' by the other, but rather the couple is seen in mutual regulation and the actions of each are seen as maintaining each other's experience and reactions. Hence it is about dysfunctional cycles: 'The more negative, narrow, and rigid these cycles, the more affect is dysregulated and the more likely the relationship is to be distressed; vice versa, the more affect is dys-regulated, the more narrow and rigid are the interactional cycles' (Greenberg & Goldman, 2008, p. 92). When dominated by such patterns, partners will no longer feel safe.

In this way the interactions can be seen as offer and counter offer. For example, Bill comes home late from work. Betty said, 'Late again! What was so important at work?' She is proposing in this interaction that she become the prosecutor and he the defendant in the ensuing interaction. This may also confirm dominance and submission. Bill might be submissive: 'Yes, you are right. There is nothing happening at work that is more important than you. I am sorry, it won't happen again'. Or Bill can adopt an attack strategy: 'I work to keep you in the manner that you have been accustomed to. How can you take the "high moral ground" when you laze around all day, waiting for me to come home so you can find something to criticise?'. Of course, these scenes are also replayed in therapy, but the psychologist has the role in EFT-C to slow down the interaction and help the couple to understand what is being played out.

Often conflict around dominance is overtly about who has the right to make decisions, but less obvious is the struggle about who has the right to define reality (Greenberg & Goldman, 2008, p. 103). This is essentially avoidance. It is too easy to focus on an external 'Late again!' when the feeling mix for Betty is loneliness, fear of abandonment and grief. Inherent in all this, Betty has denied her inner state, become focused on an external, usually with projection, and finally blaming Bill. The painful way of change for Betty must begin with her acknowledging the emotions underlying her secondary anger, to recognise her underlying vulnerabilities and powerlessness, rather than resort to attempts to control. In all this, the response of Bill can be helpful or unhelpful; the extremes of submission or counter-attack tend to 'lock in' the familiar cycle.

We can contrast the difference of invalidation:

- *Ignoring*. Bill leaves the room for his study without saying anything.
- *Criticising*. Bill to his wife: 'Why are you dressed in the same clothes you wore yesterday?'
- *Dominant defining*. Bill: 'You have no right to resent me coming home at 8 pm; you should be grateful that I work so hard.'
- *Misunderstanding*. Bill: 'You are just bitter because I forgot your birthday last week.'

And validating:

- *Understanding.* Bill: 'You expected me home a lot earlier and it is natural to be upset.'

- *Confirming.* Bill: 'I can see how upset you are, it was thoughtless of me.'

- *Respecting.* Bill: 'I can see how upset you are. I should have rung you when I realised I would be late.'

- *Attuning.* Bill: 'It is understandable that you are so upset, you were expected me home and at 6 pm and you might have been worried that something bad might have happened.'

It is the difference between what is unhealthy and healthy in relational interactions.

Summary of treatment and interventions

EFT-C has five stages of treatment (Greenberg & Goldman, 2008), each with a number of steps in the treatment process. Here is an overview of the process:

- *Stage I — Validation and alliance formation*, which involves the creation of safety and a working alliance with both partners. The steps include (a) empathising and validating the position and experience of both, especially the underlying pain of each; and (b) identifying issues of conflict and assessing how these issues reflect difficulties in connectedness and identity.

- *Stage II — Negative cycle de-escalation* in which the focus is on reducing emotional reactivity by describing the negative cycle; (c) identifying the negative interaction cycle and the role of each. Externalising the problem as the cycle; (d) identifying each partner's unacknowledged attachment or identity-related primary emotions; (e) noting the vulnerabilities and sensitivities of both and helping to better understand the negative interactional cycle (this can be assisted by understanding family-of-origin dynamics); (f) reframing the problem in terms of underlying vulnerable feelings relating to unmet needs.

- *Stage III — Accessing underlying feelings* involves actual experiencing and revealing of underlying emotions; (g) accessing unacknowledged emotions and needs underlying interactional positions; (h) identifying and overcoming mental blocks to revealing and understanding emotions; (i) promoting identification of disowned needs or aspects of the self, and integrating these into the relationship interactions.

- *Stage IV — Restructuring the negative interaction* that facilitates new ways of being with each other: (j) promoting acceptance of the partner's experience and aspects of the self; (k) expressing feelings, needs, and wishes in order to facilitate genuine emotional engagement, and restructuring the interaction by softening the blamer, distancer re-engagement, dominant going one down, and submitter asserting; (l) promoting self-soothing and transformation of maladaptive emotional schemes in each partner to facilitate personal growth and enduring change in the couple. Both may need to become more responsive to the other's needs.

- *Stage V — Consolidation and integration* in which interactional change and new narratives are supported: (m) facilitating new interactions and solutions to problematic interactions; and (n) consolidating new positions and new narratives.

There are basic negative cycles. On the affiliation dimension: pursue–distance, attack–defend, cling–push away, and demand–withdraw. These are all to do with handling closeness or emotional connection. Negative cycles on the influence dimension include: dominate–submit, lead–follow, define–defer, complain–placate, and overfunction–underfunction. There can also be mixed cycles in which one might seek closeness, but the partner wants validation. When his wife Nancy wants comfort, Karl feels like a failure because he cannot respond in a way that pleases her. She thinks that he doesn't care, so she makes critical comments. This confirms his feeling of inadequacy, so he withdraws to protect himself. This also illustrates how when Nancy feels threatened in the attachment domain she will often attack

Karl in the identity domain, so conflict arises in the realms of security and self-esteem (Greenberg & Goldman, 2008, p. 173). It is also helpful to emphasise to the couple that these cycles are not due to their deficiencies but are the result of attempted solutions that have now become the problem (Greenberg & Goldman, 2008, p. 176). There are also reciprocal cycles such as attack–attack, withdraw–withdraw and conflict related to control–control.

> *Bill:* 'I feel blamed about everything associated with my work. Betty seems irritable and impatient with me – I just can't do a thing right!'
>
> *Psychologist:* 'You want her to see the "gift" that you bring through your work, and perhaps also see you as a competent provider?' [identity needs]
>
> *Bill:* 'Yes, I really feel that I put myself out. Her comments are cutting.'
>
> *Psychologist:* 'Is it your self-esteem that is cut?'
>
> *Bill:* 'I feel hurt and wounded, bleeding in fact!'
>
> *Psychologist:* 'Maybe also humiliation?'
>
> *Bill:* 'Yes, I feel small and exposed to her comments ...'

The psychologist went on to explore the effects of shame and anger at what was experienced as a violation.

Later in the session:

> *Betty:* 'I know I am quick to anger.'
>
> *Bill:* 'Damned right!'
>
> *Psychologist, ignoring Bill's comment:* 'But is that all you feel?'
>
> *Betty more reflective:* 'I'm not sure.'
>
> *A moment later, psychologist:* 'I am sure there are some softer emotions ...'
>
> *Betty:* 'Maybe I am sad. I really miss Bill through the day and I look forward to him coming home. When he comes back late, without even a comment except being caught at work, it is as if I don't exist.'

Psychologist: 'You feel invisible?'

Betty: 'More like I don't deserve to exist.'

Later the psychologist observed: 'When Bill comes home late, a dysfunctional pattern gets played out. Sometimes — maybe often — Betty, you express anger and resentment, but maybe you first feel more sadness, in effect missing Bill, which underlies the importance of emotional connection. Bill, you often feel criticised, as if your efforts mean nothing, but it wounds you deeply in relation to feeling exposed and found wanting. Perhaps we can think together about how the pattern is defeating you both getting what you need. Perhaps creatively, together, we can construct some opportunities for a healthier interaction?'

There are some useful interventions around identifying and working with emotions. One is called 'evocative unfolding'. The psychologist asks the couple to vividly reconstruct the situation identifying stimuli, encouraging detail, and then explores the underlying emotions. Then perhaps making suggestions about what might have been experienced and then draw the link from the situation to how the couple will characteristically experience each other (see Greenberg & Goldman, 2008, pp. 201–204). There are also some suggestions to help a person to more fully experience and identify emotional reactions: clearing a space, attending to the felt sense, searching for a potential description or label, feeling shift and consolidating. There is also a guide to affirming a vulnerable state: identifying markers of the emergence of vulnerability, initial deepening, intense deepening or touching bottom, turning back to growth or hope, appreciation or reconnection with the partner, and full resolution (Greenberg & Goldman, 2008, pp. 213–214; pp. 219–220). I would also recommend a careful reading of how to work with a variety of emotions in couple therapy including anger, sadness, fear, shame and positive emotions (Greenberg & Goldman, 2008).

Susan Johnson (2004) has slightly different emphases which I think are very helpful. She consistently brings the meaning of dysfunctional patterns back to attachment styles and then employs the therapeutic technique of externalising the dysfunction to mobilise the couple to resist. A very important goal is to have 'corrective emotional experiences' in the relationship, especially in later stages of therapy to recreate a 'secure base' for the couple and their relationship.

Homework can be very helpful. This can include awareness: 'Bill, I want you to pay attention to what you feel when you are criticised'; and also expression: 'Betty, I would ask you to put into words what you want without first blaming Bill. Try to have a discussion about what might be possible'. There is a very useful homework sheet in which the couple are asked to identify in columns: situation, emotional reaction, behavioural reaction, deeper feeling and underlying need (Greenberg & Goldman, 2008, p. 161). To gain some positive experiences, the couple can be encouraged to have caring days, novel experiences, dating and holidaying. Hendrix (1988) had ideas for care behaviours, surprise behaviours and generally increasing positive interactions that I have found very helpful with couples.

As a postscript, some research in human biology suggests that there are significant differences between the male and female brain. The female brain has more interconnecting neural pathways. This leads to the hypothesis that such characteristics of the male brain may lead to men being generally are more object-centred and less able to express emotions. In contrast, women are more relational. Perhaps patterns of pursuit and distance are located in biological differences between the sexes?

Anne Moir and David Jessel (1989) concluded:

> A woman brings to the relationship emotional sensitivity, a capacity for interdependence, a yearning for companionship and for sex to reflect that emotional intimacy. A man, if not totally blind to the importance of emotions, has a less demanding emotional nature. He has the capacity for independence and sees his duties in the marital contract in terms of providing financial security. He wants a 'good' sex life, as a result of which his wife will people the small state with the family he needs ... and make solid his own foundations in life. (p. 127)

As I finish this chapter I am aware of how much more there is to say about EFT-C, and I strongly recommend a careful study of Greenberg and Goldman (2008), a text that I have relied on so heavily. Susan Johnson is the other founder of this therapy. Johnson revised *The Practice of Emotionally Focused Couple Therapy* (2004), and applied EFT-C to working with survivors of trauma (2002), which is highly recommended reading.

Chapter 6

The sexual affair

Affairs appear to be so much more common these days. Perhaps it is just that we talk about the topic more. Or do more people seek help? But regardless of any such speculation I find that affairs are often a cause of the breakdown of relationships. Sadly it seems that few people really understand what happened or are 'wiser after the event'. A few years ago I saw Andy and Margo, an attractive young couple who seemed to have everything going for them.

> Andy was a high school teacher and he had an infatuation with Kirsty, another teacher in his school. Kirsty had recently separated from her husband and Andy was 'being supportive'. Margo was in a state of near panic and she acutely felt the threat of Kirsty to their marriage.

It is difficult to know how to take statistics, but one interesting trend is that younger wives are now more unfaithful than their husbands, two thirds of women and half of men who were having affairs were in the first five years of marriage (Lawson, 1988). Until a couple of decades ago men were more likely to have an affair, but now the genders are about equal. However, if a man is unfaithful he is more likely to have more sexual partners. There are a lot of potential factors in all this, such as higher expectations of emotional fulfilment in marriage, the general absence of relationship and communication skills with many couples, changes in what is acceptable in society, and the changing structure of our lives, including a greater proportion of married women in employment.

Almost all people enter a romantic relationship, whether marriage or living together, with a conscious intention of remaining sexually faithful. So an affair is inevitably a falling from an initial ideal, whether a religious or a personal value. It is usually secretive, guilt inducing in the person involved and anywhere from infuriating to shattering when the partner finds out. Although most of this chapter will focus on the affair in relation to a marriage, the dynamics are similar for an engagement, de facto partnership, or longer-term committed relationship. In these cases there may be less of a public dimension with vows made in a marriage service and the legal situation may be less entangled, though children are often directly involved.

A symptom

While affairs may be erotic and intensely sexual, there is a sense in which they have little to do with sex. The real dynamics are unexplored conflict, anger, fear and emptiness. Such is the pain of an unhappy relationship that an affair tries to keep at bay. It is the symptom of a deeper malaise. An example:

> Will and Marg have been married eight years. There has not been much 'sparkle' in their relationship for quite a while. Will became attracted to a colleague and what began as a few drinks after work ended up with sexual involvement. Will is now less troubled by Marg's emotional coldness, and the affair has drained away some of the tension from the marriage. This is a false calm before the emotional storm when Marg finds out about the relationship.

This example illustrates the principle that an affair almost always represents an externalisation of an unhealthy process in the original relationship. Thus the affair may help to keep the real issues, such as unresolved conflict over differing needs, 'safely' underground.

In many ways the affair is in a 'fairy land' of unreality. The relationship begins with excitement, compelling attraction and the thrill of 'forbidden fruits'. But it is a protected relationship:

> It does not have the everyday worries and chores of marriage or
> the pressures of living intimately with another person over time. It
> is a hidden relationship, shared only with one or two confidants
> who are chosen for their ability to be supportive and to keep the
> secret. The secrecy provides a shell against outside pressures.
> (Brown, 1991, p. 24)

The marriage still impinges on the affair: the spouse still comes
first in finances, family crises and celebrations, and in public.
So the unfaithful partner becomes torn between competing
demands, especially as the other person becomes more impatient.

If we are to understand the dynamics of an affair, the larger
picture of the family is important. This includes the children, the
respective families-of-origin, and behaviour patterns of near relatives, as well as what is considered permissible in the wider
ethnic group (cf. the affair labelled the 'Irish divorce', which is
seemingly tolerated by the French). The family-of-origin, for
example, can leave an adult with 'unfinished business'. There
may be patterns of avoidance, seduction, secrecy, and betrayal.
The precedent for turning away from relationship difficulties and
escaping into an affair may be set within the generations. It
becomes so much easier as the pattern repeats. It is a two-way
street: an affair is the result of various dynamics in the family and,
of course, will influence others with or without the 'discovery'.

The family is a primary place of belonging. An affair threatens
the glue that holds everything together and therefore the very
basis of belonging. It arouses and fuels the fear of abandonment.
No wonder emotions run hot!

The nature of the affair

The couple will tend to respond in very different ways:

> For the spouse, the betrayal seems unbearable. Yet for the unfaithful
> partner the affair is an aphrodisiac. The aura of romance and
> intrigue is compelling, especially when reality feels barren or
> boring. Affairs promise so much: an opportunity to pursue dreams
> that have been dormant, to come alive again, to find someone who
> truly understands. Their hidden promise is pain. (Brown, 1991, p. 2)

The destructive aspect of an affair was spelt out in Proverbs long ago: 'For a prostitute's fee is only a loaf of bread, but the wife of another stalks a man's very life. Can fire be carried in the bosom without burning one's clothes?' (Prov. 6:26–27).

Involvement in the affair can be sexual, emotional or both. Women are more likely to be emotionally involved. The combination of sexual and emotional elements represents more of a threat to the marriage than either alone. Some generalisations might be made about gender in marital dissatisfaction: women tend to see sex as flowing from intimacy; whereas, men see it as a path to intimacy. Therefore, it is natural that women's dissatisfaction will most often come from emotional issues, while males will complain about of lack of sex. This would generally support my clinical impression that when the woman has an affair it is usually more ominous for the future of the relationship.

Depression may be a factor and this should be carefully assessed. Mid-life issues can add another dimension of potential complications. So often the conclusion is reached after yet another unresolved fight: 'This is not where I belong!'

An affair is most likely at the following times in the marriage:

- early in the marriage when the partners are struggling with issues of commitment and intimacy
- when the first or second child arrives and motherhood becomes the focus for the wife or house-husband
- when children leave home
- when it becomes clear that no matter what is done the partner will not conform to the idealised image.

Emily Brown (1991) identified six stages in the affair: First, there is a period of creating a climate in which an affair can happen. Conflict is avoided and issues are not discussed. The level of dissatisfaction may become high in the marriage. Both feel stuck. Second is the act of betrayal. One of the partners will become involved in an affair. There may be some suspicions but the guilty one tends to deny that there is anything wrong and the spouse tries hard not to see what may be obvious. Sometimes there is a seemingly paranoid phase in which the spouse obsesses about every hint of another person. The third stage is the discovery of the affair. Sometimes the guilt is so great that he or she will confess. A friend may know about the affair and tell the spouse. Perhaps most common is the discovery of evidence that is unmistakable, such as hotel receipts or long-distance phone records. Usually this is validation, and possibly a huge relief: 'I knew that something was wrong. I am not crazy!' This is a major turning point in which the couple will not see themselves in the same light again — to some extent, the relationship has lost its innocence.

Gottman (1999) described the distance and isolation cascade, which is characterised by flooding (of emotions), seeing problems as severe, believing that it is best to work out problems alone, leading parallel lives and loneliness (p. 72). It is hardly surprising that as a person descends this cascade they will be more open to having an affair. However, while an option, an affair is never a solution. When a relationship is happy other potential relationships do not look attractive or seem unduly risky and costly. If the relationship is failing then other relationships start looking good (p. 73).

Brown (1991) also offers the model of what she has identified as the five different kinds of affairs.

CONFLICT AVOIDANCE AFFAIRS
In this kind of affair there is a shout: 'I'll make you pay attention to me!' Sometimes a couple will have a 'nice' relationship, like a pond with hardly a surface ripple. Every difference of viewpoint is avoided and eventually this 'peace' becomes suffocating. Usually the more dissatisfied spouse gets into the affair and then manages to get quickly 'found out'. The discovery takes the covers off problems in the relationship. It is a 'relief' to have things out in the open.

This kind of affair usually happens in the early years of the relationship, and it becomes a signal to work on the issues that have been buried. The affair may occur in what everyone thinks is a model marriage.

But this is a facade. Negative feelings have been long repressed, with resentment the emotion closest to awareness. There may also be an underlying depression. The affair is rarely a serious relationship as the purpose is to get the spouse's attention. This kind of affair is very common among those who may have been taught — or come to the conclusion — that anger is bad and must be avoided at all costs.

The threat to the marriage is more in the avoidance of conflict than the affair. There is hope for the relationship if the couple are willing to face underlying issues. Ending the marriage or quickly forgiving are both 'cop-outs'. The straying spouse will most commonly ring the psychologist, and this is the only kind of affair in which he or she is likely to express much guilt. The guilty person will often be mystified by their own behaviour, saying something like: 'I don't know what got into me'.

> Rob confessed the next day to Marlene: 'I have no idea what happened. I have no particular feelings for Sally. We were both at the conference, and after-dinner drinks led to, well you know. I feel so guilty — and I promise never to see her again — can you just forgive me? I want to make things right.' Marlene was certainly prepared to forgive Rob, but she realised that something was wrong in their marriage.
>
> I saw them a week later. Rob and Marlene had only a vague sense of dissatisfaction in their relationship. It was puzzling: 'Why the affair?' But they soon began to realise that underneath the avoiding of 'hot issues', even just 'warm issues', there was deep dissatisfaction. After the violation of the relationship Marlene found it easier to be angry. Rob was obsessed with his guilt, but gradually he too was able to express resentment, especially about Marlene's frequent unwillingness for sex. After about six sessions, I thought that Rob and Marlene now had an opportunity to build a relationship based on better communication and conflict resolution.

INTIMACY AVOIDANCE AFFAIRS

All affairs reveal problems in intimacy. However, in this kind of relationship the avoidance of intimacy is central. This affair is a shield against hurt and disappointment, with a barely conscious message: 'I don't want to need you so much, so I'll get some of my needs met elsewhere'. It is easier to argue than to be vulnerable and risk intimacy.

Intimacy avoiders appear to be very good at fighting. Whether it is hot or icy, conflict is endless. Exchanges are filled with criticism, sarcasm, and blame. The mutual hostility may provide a justification for turning to someone else. The affair then becomes a weapon in the fight and the partner may counter with another affair. One of clearest indicators of this type of affair is when both spouses are involved in affairs. It is perhaps predictable that such affairs usually provide little genuine intimacy.

The way the couple stay in contact is through conflict, but paradoxically the anger gives the safety of distance as well. The bond, through 'push–pull', can be amazingly strong. It is easy to justify the affair when there may be quite abusive conflict. Expressions of guilt are rare even after the discovery of the affair. Under the surface there is a great deal of pain and fear. It is dance in which both want the assurance of the other's love.

This kind of affair may occur early in the marriage. At this stage the couple usually still care about each other. Early goodwill may help in getting over initial difficulties. The issues, however, are more complex than with *conflict avoiders*. The hidden problems usually originate in childhood experiences and the partners are left with a fear of getting too close. Conflict has a lot of energy; though this may be mostly negative it can be beneficial. These couples are usually not afraid of conflict and can discuss sensitive issues openly — although who is in control is usually a powerful issue. Sometimes I will help the couple with communication skills and assist them to express their feelings in a more productive way. In this way intimacy needs can begin to be met in the relationship, but steps to intimacy should proceed slowly.

If the issues around vulnerability and dependency are not addressed then affairs can become a way of life. The 'open marriage' is a variation of this theme of intimacy avoidance. Ironically, for both conflict and intimacy avoidance affairs there is a deep bond felt by both partners in the marriage.

Val called me early in the morning asking for an emergency session. She had been referred by an agency with a long waiting list. She asked: 'Can I see you first? I have just found out that my husband has been seeing prostitutes when he is overseas.' I told her that if the issue was their relationship I preferred to see them together, but she would have an opportunity to speak briefly with me alone. I then fitted them in at the end of the day.

There was high tension in their relationship. It was hard to get the story straight, but eventually it came out that Paul had caught a venereal disease when he was last in the Philippines. The recriminations had continued with mutual blame and Val called after an incidence of violence.

The relationship was entangled and surprisingly strong for all the mutual blame. Neither raised the issue of leaving and I quickly engaged both in the counselling process. Once they were calmer I was able to begin to work on how they spoke to each other. They were able to face issues directly and though at times were savage with each other began to make some real contact. I asked them to talk about their experiences growing up and this led to some deep insights. In Val's home the parents were continually in an uproar. In contrast, Paul's parents never spoke to each other. There was a constant tension between two people who appeared to be strangers. Gradually Paul and Val realised that they had no training in communicating at a deep level. They resolved to use an egg timer as a symbol of when they would have a 'deep and meaningful'. After about ten sessions they had made such progress that they wanted to see if they could make it on their own. And last I heard from them they were happily together.

SEXUAL ADDICTION AFFAIRS

The 'womaniser' or 'temptress' is a special case. This kind of person avoids dealing with personal needs by making conquests, perhaps with the expressed hope of finding 'true love'.

Such individuals usually come from a deprived past, sometimes with abuse or suffering neglect, and experience themselves as empty — nothing fills them up in a lasting way. The conquests compensate for feelings of isolation, shame, and low self-esteem. It is addictive behaviour, being compulsive and seemingly out of control. It usually continues in spite of the cost. This can also be a pattern with patients who have a personality disorder or strong traits (see Chapter 8).

I have seen a number of these people in counselling, usually males, and I experience an urge to tell them 'to grow up' (which I would never express). They often have an adolescent quality, expressed in bragging about conquests. Risk may be something of a 'narcotic hit'. Perhaps the only hope of change is through providing a measure of re-parenting with extended psychotherapy.

In this type of affair the lover is usually of little significance, though there may be surface qualities, such as attractive looks or power of position. It is safe to predict that there will be many partners over time and these will never be enough. Such affairs tend to happen throughout the marriage. Often there is a defiance, a sort of 'catch me if you can'. I remember a musician telling me he was just addicted to 'recreational sex'. Also, I have been placed in the farcical situation of the wife sending the errant husband to be 'fixed'.

The spouse may be prepared to overlook the affairs and be satisfied with an empty shell of a marriage. One model of understanding the spouse of the sexual addict is co-dependency. According to Carnes (2007), co-dependents tend to make three mistakes: (1) mistake intensity for intimacy, (2) obsession for care, and (3) control for security. There are usually elements of de-selfing as well.

It is not easy to help the sexual addict. As a psychologist I have found it best to confront them in a supportive way and together work out the emotional needs being 'met'. It may be tempting to be judgmental, but this increases shame and denial; instead it is important to connect with the addict's dislike of his or her own behaviour and desire for a better relationship. Motivational interviewing, which has been found to be effective with alcohol and drug dependency, can be used and I think offers what might be an effective evidence-based therapy (EBT). If the individual is reasonably motivated, and is committed to working through the issues from childhood, then there is some possibility of change. But frankly, this is uncommon.

Nicholas came to see me after his new wife threatened to leave him. She found out that he 'made a pass' at one of her close friends. He was in his late twenties, tall with an athletic build. He was very engaging and quite charming.

Nicholas: 'I think I need some help or I'll lose this marriage the way I lost my last one.'

Psychologist: 'So you want to make some changes.'

Nicholas: 'I guess that's right. I kept getting entangled in affairs with friends, neighbours, or work colleagues. I can't blame Kylie for eventually leaving me. I wanted to make this relationship better with Bess, but I have 'screwed up' again. Oh, I didn't actually get in bed with Sally but it was only because she said no.'

Psychologist: 'So you began the marriage with Bess with fidelity in mind in spite of your past record?'

Nicholas: 'For years I justified my behaviour by telling myself that Kylie couldn't satisfy me sexually. I think she half believed that as well, but eventually she refused to take that responsibility. Perfectly reasonable I suppose?'

Psychologist: 'Yes, indeed.'

Nicholas: 'Now I feel like I'm in the same rut again with Bess, I think that I have to admit that the problem is really me.'

Psychologist: 'I'm glad that you have come to that realisation. It makes our work together possible.'

In the next three months Nicholas proved to be very motivated. His mother was an alcoholic who had never married and he came to realise that his emptiness was related to a lack of nurture when he was a child. Perhaps in some way she felt as empty and tried to fill that intense need with her addiction. Bess was very helpful in the process in holding him accountable and keeping lines of communication open.

It is helpful to understand the principle of 'change talk' from motivational interviewing, which encourages the psychologist to position himself or herself in such a way that the patient is encouraged to talk about change. This is illustrated in the following:

Psychologist: 'So as I understand it, you like the excitement of the chase and novelty of different partners. But you have found some heavy costs as well. What do you see as the main disadvantages?'

Nicholas: 'I think it is the Alfie syndrome, I always end up alone and full of regrets.'

Psychologist: 'And?'

Nicholas: 'I end up losing my self-respect and I want to build something lasting in terms of a relationship …'

EMPTY-NEST AFFAIRS

The empty-nest affair signals a marriage held together by a belief in family, rather than a strong emotional bond. It is the typical family man, married 20 years, who will now admit that he has never really loved his wife. Or he will say that he had doubts since the beginning, but went ahead anyway. It would appear that he de-selfed while trying to make 'a go of it' and have a successful marriage. But having said this, there are an equal number of wives who have filled exactly that role for a decade or two and now look elsewhere for intimacy.

The marriage may have been a matter of status or convenience. While the children are still at home the focus is on them. When it becomes obvious that the marriage is empty, he or she is tempted to seek fulfilment elsewhere. It is the relationship rather than the individual that is empty. Communication may be limited to purely practical matters.

Sometimes there was deprivation in the family-of-origin. This person was initially motivated to have a better family. It may lead to the myth of the perfect marriage. The dark side is pushed out of awareness, feelings are excluded, and amazingly this can work for many years. Sometimes there is a deep commitment to religious values. The ideal is all important.

The affair tends to be a serious matter and can last for years. The partner in the affair then becomes idealised, with the spouse devalued. Participants tend to be more discreet and do not invite discovery. However, when it is revealed it can be deeply wounding to the partner, especially if that individual believes that the marriage is not over.

Sometimes the affair is part of what might be labelled a 'midlife crisis', when typically a man becomes involved with a much younger woman. Perhaps the timing is later with a 'last chance affair'. The identifying phrase may be 'I don't love you' and this indicates, at least in my experience, that for this person the relationship has been dead for years. The outlook for the marriage is usually poor. By now the marital partners know only each other's public self and it is usually too late to create a satisfying emotional attachment.

There is usually some reluctance to enter counselling. But if there is willingness, I have found it useful to focus on issues in the family-of-origin. Typically this involves understanding, disentangling both partners' feelings, needs, goals and backgrounds. Once this process is underway, forgiveness may become possible (Gordon & Baucom, 1988). Sometimes I have seen the couple as individuals for a while, with marital counselling following later. Sadly, a typical motive for seeking counselling is to leave the abandoned spouse in the care of the psychologist.

> James saw me only at the demand of his wife, Fiona. He explained to me: 'I really have no energy to work on the marriage. It is pointless. Fiona has finally found out about my relationship with Michelle, and I suppose that clarifies things for me. I want to move to Sydney so I can be with her. Our son Mike

has nearly finished his law degree and he can come to see me on the odd weekend.'

OUT-THE-DOOR AFFAIRS

The erring spouse is seriously thinking about ending the marriage. So this affair is an attempt to answer such questions as 'Can I make it on my own?', 'Am I still attractive?', 'Can I be happy in another relationship?', and most important, 'Can I get you to kick me out?' The purpose has two aspects. There is usually a quest for self-validation, but less consciously there may also be a desire to avoid taking responsibility for ending the marriage. The affair is a distraction from the difficulties and the pain of ending the marriage.

The other person is usually portrayed as 'understanding'. The relationship may have been built on a close friendship. He or she is someone to talk with about marital dissatisfactions and hopes for the future. The affair confirms that the marriage is unsatisfactory and this justifies the impending separation. The unfaithful spouse will usually ensure that they are 'found out', and sometimes they are disappointed that even then the spouse will not end the marriage. Sometimes the outside person is blamed as 'the evil one', but this is something of a smokescreen that protects the couple from feeling responsible for the state of the relationship. Sometimes the spouse will marry the other person, trying to justify the affair, but this only further avoids the real issues and builds the new relationship upon a very shaky foundation. The task of counselling is difficult as the unfaithful spouse may only be coming to self-justify: 'I did everything that I could'. Usually the spouse being left is more willing to face issues such as the loss of the marriage and adjustment to a different life. There may be some need to improve communication, which will help them in facing their parenting responsibilities.

Generally the prognosis for the marriage gets worse as the assessment moves from conflict avoidance to out-the-door affairs. It is helpful when both can accept responsibility for creating the unhappy nature of the marriage, and a psychologist can help to define the underlying nature of the problems in the relationship. Rebuilding takes time, whether it is focused on the marriage or on the future after separation. Sometimes forgiveness is possible and it has a healing effect.

> Trudi had married Laurie, a successful medical specialist who was about 15 years older. They had two children in their marriage. Trudi was initially very reluctant to tell her husband about the affair with Frank.
>
> *Trudi:* 'I can't bear to tell him. I know it will hurt him terribly. Frank is actually a year older than Laurie. I know it sounds silly but I think he could understand if I left for a younger man.'
>
> *Psychologist:* 'So you intend to leave?'
>
> *Trudi:* 'Yes I will leave, but I am not really in love with Frank. I may see with him for a little while but I really want to get on with my life.'

THE HOMOSEXUAL AFFAIR

I would like to add another category to Brown's five types of affairs. It is the affair with a gay lover. There are some similarities with the out-the-door affair because the prognosis is usually poor for the marriage. But it also has elements of the empty nest in which there may be a deep attachment to the lover.

There are differences with the apparent change in orientation. Some people are aware of attraction to a same-sex partner in their teens but hold back for reasons of personal, family or social disapproval. The social stigma may lead to trying to make a marriage work. Moral values or religious beliefs may also add to the determination to make a success of a traditional marriage. This resolve can later break down.

> Bennie experimented with some homosexual encounters when he was a teenager. He tried to dismiss it as 'sexual exploration' until he found the urge to visit gay bars irresistible. He had a troubled marriage and when his wife found out about his homosexual activity she left him and refused to speak to him

except through her lawyer. He was confused and somewhat ashamed of his desires: 'I can't understand it. I still only want to have a steady relationship with a woman, but I go for casual sex through a gay bar.'

In some cases there is a more recent attraction and this can be very confusing.

Mark rang me in a state of panic. He had found out that his wife had a female lover. On the phone he poured out: 'Damn it! We have four children, all teenagers, how the hell could this have happened?'

Gabrielle came in for the first session. Mark sent her hoping that I would change her back.

Gabrielle: 'I met Angie at church. We both help with a coffee house ministry. It involves outreach to the unemployed. We began with being good friends.'

Psychologist: 'But soon it seemed …'

Gabrielle: 'She made the first approach. I suppose we hugged a lot initially, but now we are lovers. I was surprised but I soon found myself deeply attracted to her. I mean I am a mother and all that …'

Psychologist: 'So it has been hard to come to terms with?'

Gabrielle: 'The thought of Mark touching me disgusts me. I can no longer sleep in the same room and I think it is hopeless staying together for our children. This sounds like I have made up my mind to leave, doesn't it?'

Psychologist: 'Yes.'

Gabrielle had some theological conflicts to resolve but as far as she was concerned the marriage was over.

The rejection of the partner is possibly the hardest to bear in this kind of affair. As Mark later said: 'It is not just me personally. I could understand it if she went with another man, but a woman? She is so "turned off" that she is rejecting my gender as well, how could I fail her like that?'

A note about triangles

Affairs have been called the 'eternal triangle'. In Bowen's theory the concept of triangles is relevant. In this the pattern, not the person, becomes the problem. It is a systems way of thinking.

I try to help couples to deal with rigid triangles by:

- keeping conflict focused on the issue. It helps to deal directly with the conflict in the relationship where it belongs and not to displace anger onto someone else.
- avoiding using a child, even a grown-up one, as a 'marital therapist' or go-between
- distinguishing between respect for privacy and 'playing secrets'. Gossip and secrets encourage triangles because such behaviour requires that two or more persons conspire to exclude another or others.
- keeping lines of communication open without inviting others to blame or take sides in battles.

The rules of 'de-fusing' a triangle are: stay calm (anxiety and intense emotions drive triangles); stay out (leave the other two to manage their own relationship: no advising, helping, criticising, blaming, fixing, lecturing, analysing, and so on); and keep in emotional contact with the other two people. This is more difficult when the triangle involves an affair, because the crisis dominates the climate of the relationship. This may be more possible in conflict and intimacy avoidance affairs, but difficult in the more complex dynamics of the others.

One advantage of working with a systems model of family therapy is that it enables me to see whoever is willing to make changes. Self-focus can be encouraged and small changes can be made that can have quite profound effects in the family system. It should not be forgotten that the psychologist in marital therapy is quickly triangulated into the marital relationship. This is natural and gives me the opportunity to model effective de-triangulating moves by maintaining both neutrality and emotional connectedness with both parties.

Repair if possible

EFT-C understands an affair as attachment trauma. It is of course natural for the betrayed partner to be 'shell shocked' and find trust almost impossible. An affair, because it is so traumatic, can almost mimic posttraumatic stress disorder (PTSD) with common symptoms such as 'obsessive thoughts, flashbacks or intrusive thoughts, numbness and detachment, hyperarousal, and hypervigilance. Obsessive thoughts about what happened will only dissipate when shattered assumptions about the relationship are addressed and an alternate narrative has been constructed about the affair' (Greenberg & Goldman, 2008, p. 289). It may be important to validate the injured partner's need for a 'protective wall', and to carefully explore the unique meaning of what has happened. Naturally this will happen at every level, including the emotional aftermath. If there is a desire to continue working on the relationship, the offending partner may have to let go of the expectation that their partner will forgive, 'forget' and trust again. This will not happen in a hurry — if ever. It is helpful if the offending partner can acknowledge and demonstrate feelings associated with guilt and shame. At the right time, when the betrayed partner can, forgiveness is a very powerful and healing step for the relationship (Gordon & Baucom, 1988).

Summary

An affair is not the most common reason for a relationship ending. Some research would indicate that close to 80% of people leaving a marriage say that the reason for getting divorced is gradually growing apart. Affairs as the reason were cited by about 20% to 27% (Gigy & Kelly, as cited in Gottman, 1999, p. 23). It is symptomatic of the gradual deterioration of a relationship that makes one or both vulnerable to 'going outside' to meet emotional needs. A useful reference for couples is Janis Spring's *After the Affair*, published in 1996.

In the end, an affair may not be completely destructive. Sometimes the relationship survives and grows stronger —

although usually both partners hurt terribly, the affair may indicate that they want something more in the relationship. The dream for the relationship may have ended, but reality can yet be satisfying and rewarding. And even the in wake of a broken relationship, there is the possibility of insight and being wiser the next time around.

Chapter 7

Sex therapy: The scope and the challenges

The ability to have a satisfying sexual relationship is important to almost every adult. Yet, perhaps surprisingly, it is only briefly mentioned in most clinical psychology programs across Australia. Certainly this is the case in Canberra, Australia. In preparing this chapter, I rang the Australian Psychological Society and I was told that no specific record of this kind of training is kept by the association. It is also important to note that Medicare rebates are paid for sessions that address sexual problems for patients referred by general practitioners to clinical psychologists under mental health care plans.

One of the issues for clinicians, particularly early in their careers, is the lack of comfort around enquiring about our clients' sexual wellbeing or discussing in detail the complaints they bring to our attention. This is a normal developmental issue according to Fonagy (2008). He is an attachment-focused psychoanalyst who advocates normal sexual education in families. He observed that sexual development and experience is seldom if ever discussed in detail and that this area of our functioning remains mysterious, unattended to, unnamed or unmentionable, uninformed, unregulated and unreflected upon until we find ourselves in an intimate physical relationship. Even then, many people, despite having sexual relationships, never discuss their experience with their partners. Only then do we have a chance with another to claim our sexuality. Perhaps there is a parallel between developmental taboos of talking about sexuality and the lack of information provided in the training of clinical psychologists? There is a clear need for remedy.

It is a good principle in sex therapy, as in other treatments, to start by dealing with the most immediate and straightforward issues. I will first list the type of sexual issues and concerns that have arisen in my clinical practice. This will not include a detailed treatment of approaches that are well documented elsewhere. Second, I will outline some of the issues that are specific to sex therapy, issues that overlap with but are not the same as those emerging during couples' therapy. Then three models are introduced to help organise the approaches one might take from simple problems to more complex. A complex case will be presented, which illustrates how various levels of intervention may be involved in the treatment of a couple's sexual difficulties. And last, I will review the topics I believe clinicians need to be familiar with and desirable areas of knowledge for those aspiring to be effective in sex therapy.

Typical problems

The sexual difficulties most commonly brought to therapists working with relationships include lack of sexual knowledge, primary anorgasmia (women who have never experienced orgasm), premature ejaculation for men (often both partners have difficulties and these are often found together), and difference of desire for couples. The latter problem is rampant; in fact, most couples experience this at some time in their sex lives. Fortunately, the most well researched and robust treatment approaches exist for these issues and are well described in the popular self-help literature (Heiman & LoPiccolo, 1988; King, 1998, 1999; Kashack & Tiefer, 2002; Zilbergeld, 1999). Problems of a couple dealing with under- or over-amounts of desire, arousal, and orgasm are also present. At times people present faking desire or arousal to hide underlying difficulties. Faking orgasm is common occurrence for women, but I had one male client with serious, life-long retarded ejaculation who also pretended ejaculation and climax, afraid to reveal possible infertility (cf. Leiblum, 2007).

The range of concern is vast and includes the following: life cycle specific issues (pregnancy, postpartum, menopause, postmenopause, prostate difficulties), teenage or later body image and comfort as a sexual person. Sexual issues arise due to relationship crises such as affairs, domestic violence, and grief. Religious and cultural norms, values and beliefs influence sexual function and can be particularly salient the lives of cross cultural couples. The internet has increased the access to pornography and the incidence of 'internet' infidelity and sexual addiction. People can feel betrayed by their partner's use of visual pornography on a single occasion all the way to a repetitive and increasing use of pornography. At times people develop internet affairs with others talking on chat lines, which can lead to physical affairs (Abrams Spring, 1996; Brown 1991; Watts 2009). Although not all affairs affect a couple's sexual functioning (paradoxically an affair can stimulate sexual activity and increase satisfaction in the couple's relationship), the resulting lack of trust can affect the most robust of libidos. Couples present where one partner is crossdressing, has transvestite aspects, or has had a sex-change operation. Same-sex couples both resemble and differ from heterosexual couples. The choice of same- or opposite-gender therapist, or gay or straight therapist can have meaning and impact on the therapy and may often be usefully explored.

Health issues (e.g., cardiac disease, diabetes, vulvodynea, sexually transmitted diseases), mental health disorders (e.g., anxiety, depression), disabilities (e.g., chronic pain, spinal and other orthopaedic injuries), pharmacological (e.g., alcohol, antidepressant medication) and other treatment effects (e.g., fertility treatment) all can cause sexual problems (Schnarch, 2002), and do emerge in clinical practice alongside other presenting problems.

An unfortunate number of couples are sexually affected by the after effects of trauma resulting from childhood sexual abuse or rape. This is an area in which patients often present as individuals wanting to resolve issues on their own before possibly involving a partner. Trauma work can be very useful and, with lesser trauma, partner involvement in treatment is not always necessary for full resolution of sexual difficulties. Several women I have worked with have addressed posttraumatic stress disorder (PTSD) symptoms resulting from rape in short-term therapy. Eye movement desensitisation and reprocessing (EMDR; Shapiro, 1989) has often been a very efficient approach particularly for women who have had 'simple' or once-off traumatic events. After treatment, reminders of the abuse no longer trigger unpleasant emotions and disrupt intercourse with a current partner. For other women the effects of longer, systematic, cruel and repeated abuse may never be resolved. The therapeutic task is for these patients to attain their maximum possible functioning, grieve and accept they will have to live with the irretrievable effects of the trauma. The presence of a third party in the relationship is even more challenging for couples discussing the most physically intimate aspects of their lives. This adds a dimension of difficulty to normal couple therapy.

Beginning treatment

The best strategy as a treating psychologist is to be tentative, assess the couple's comfort levels in starting the discussion of sexual material, adopt the couples' language, ask permission at each step of asking for more intimate or graphic information ('I would like to get details about your love making. Is it OK with you if we proceed in this way now?'), but to titrate this to their level of comfort. It is also good practice to know about the partner's sexual physical health, with input from a general practitioner and/or gynaecologist. Different medical issues can arise for people who are at the beginning of their sexual lives and who have not yet been able to function fully, than for people who have lost sexual function. It is important to know a person's physical circumstances before embarking on psychological or relationship treatment. The complex case outlined at the end of this chapter will illustrate the type of challenges treatment can face due to health conditions. Gender, age, sexual preference, cultural, racial or religious differences between the psychologist and the couple are best respectfully articulated so that they have a chance to voice and deal with any discomfort from the start of therapy. It is possible that referral to another psychologist might be advisable.

The three models that I have found useful are the King model, the permission, limited information, specific suggestions and intensive therapy (PLISSIT) model, and the Bernal and Baker multi-level intervention model. Each will be outlined and illustrated by a clinical case. This combination fits with Lebow's (1997) notion of an integrative approach to working with couples.

The King model (1998) simply states that for a couple to have a satisfactory sexual relationship the partners have to have a reasonably positive view of *self* + *sex* + *body* +*partner* + *relationship* + *environment*. This view quickly helps the treating psychologist get a picture in which two individuals' issues lie in sex therapy. Assessing both areas of strength as well as areas of need for both parties is essential.

To proceed in therapy it is also best for a couple to gain a good enough rapport, commitment to the relationship, positive mutual feelings, absence or low level of the four predictors of relationship failure (contempt, criticism, stonewalling, defensiveness) according to Gottman (1999), as well as general comfort with touch treatment, and as well as a sufficient capacity for psychological insight and self-reflection.

The PLISSIT model (Annon, 1976) is a straightforward way of grouping various sex therapy interventions, with its four increasingly more complex levels:

1. *Permission.* In this area individuals or couples are encouraged to be open and develop comfort and trust in revealing and

discussing sexual areas of their lives and relationship. Information about what is normal sexual functioning fits into this section.

2. *Limited information.* Here individuals or couples are given specific but limited information, and maybe ideas of strategies to use applied to their specific concerns.

3. *Specific suggestions.* These tend to be approaches or interventions based on more in-depth familiarity with the details of sexual difficulties and specifically tailored to these.

4. *Intensive therapy.* This would be applied to complex cases in which more in-depth individual or couple therapy and/or many different approaches are needed and contribute to treatment of a longer-term nature.

In the case presented later, all levels were used and woven throughout the therapy.

The Bernal and Baker model (1979) has five levels:

1. *Problem level* — for example, 'sex'.

2. *Individual level* — one of us, preferably 'you', is at fault or both of us are 'defective'.

3. *Transactional level* — we misunderstand each other or our communication, conflict management and decision-making skills are ineffective.

4. *Relationship level* — rules, roles, patterns are restrictive.

5. *Contextual level* — family-of-origin, treatment setting, culture, socioeconomic circumstances (Arnstein, 1988, Bernal & Baker, 1979). Clients who become stuck in one view of their difficulties can benefit from a shift to considering them in one or more of the others. Understanding individuals or couples in any of these dimensions can be liberating for the couple. The young couple from McEwan's (2007) novel *On Chesil Beach*, in which the partners did not consummate their marriage, can be useful in illustrating these options.

First, we would assess their problem as sexual. The couple needs a great deal of information about what is normal sexuality and permission to talk about themselves, their relationship and sex. The second level, individual therapy, might be recommended to each of them to deal with the legacy of their traumatic and emotionally distant families, their individual attitudes, beliefs and fears about themselves as individuals and about the opposite sex. Focusing specifically on sex, one might look at the way each partner learned about sex in their families, how they perceived their parents' sexual relationships, how touch and physical affection featured in their upbringings. The third level, the transactional level, is where communication skills would be assessed, in particular their knowledge, comfort and style of interacting about sex. Teaching or coaching them in this area would be the approach. In the fourth level, the relationship level, a new rule might be suggested in which communicating about family history, as well as sexuality and emotions was allowable. In the fifth level, the contextual level, Framo (1982) suggests separate family-of-origin sessions might be used, with the respective spouses meeting with parents and/or siblings to discuss and understand the origin and effects of many of these issues, to correct misperceptions and open up new ways of interacting for the couple with each other as well as with their respective families.

I will use the work with 'Polly' and 'Ray' to illustrate the usefulness of the models discussed earlier. The material that follows is inspired by a real case, but is not presented in chronologically complete clinical detail.

Ray, referred by a younger female colleague, presented as the husband in a mature couple married for about two years, who said they had not been able to consummate their marriage and develop the comfortable sexual relationship they both had hoped for. He was in his late 50s and Polly was about five years younger. He was retired and she was still enjoying her work. Both had been previously married with two married adult children each. Ray had had intervening relationships, one of which had ended very badly and he had been badly used financially. Polly, he said, seemed to have been traumatised by her ex-husband, a violent man who left her, taking most of the family assets. After a platonic courtship of several years they had married on a culturally significant date. Polly, living in Australia since the early days of her first marriage, was of Asian origin and this was an important practice in her country. Ray had consented to this timing, though he was covertly concerned that physically this was not the best time for him as he had recently had spinal surgery and was still convalescing. He had not articulated, either to himself or to Polly, these possible limitations before their nuptials. During their honeymoon, their attempts at sexual intercourse had failed, leaving each feeling misunderstood, unattractive and a failure. Attempts to bridge this gap ended in bitter circular fights, leaving both feeling increasingly unhappy, bitter, lonely and disappointed. Ray's back improved and he wanted their sexual relationship to improve. He blamed her in large part for not understanding the impact of his physical problems as well as suspecting she carried trauma effects from her first marriage. After trying one therapist Polly was reluctant to speak to another but had sent a detailed letter of her view with Ray when he came to the first session alone.

Within the King model (1998) of good sexual relating based on both partners' positive views of *self + sex + body + partner + relationship + environment*, already Polly and Ray presented as having difficulty: self (Ray's health issues, Polly with possible trauma, both with respective past relationship disappointments and betrayals, both with likely low self-esteem as desirable partners); sex (marriage not consummated); body (Ray with failure to get an erection); partner (blaming of each other for their problems); relationship (the lack of sexual closeness, and the fights with members of the opposite sex). Problems about their environment, children and families, the tug of loyalties and different family dynamics were mentioned, but will not be covered here.

The first task was to invite Polly to attend joint therapy in person with Ray in order to get her views. He expressed a preference for a few individual sessions in which he described his history. During these sessions I wondered out loud if Polly might be more comfortable with an older female therapist who was also a migrant. I also suggested to Ray, King's (1998) book *Good Loving, Great Sex,* in the hope of conveying to both Ray and Polly that our process would be nonblaming and focused on both of their needs as well as their interactions. In session 6, Polly joined us and remained as a part of the therapy. Most of our work was done with both of them present, but sometimes there were individual sessions as the need arose. There was success in addressing some of the issues. They met the preconditions for sex therapy: they said they loved each other and were basically committed to their marriage. They had enjoyed affection and touch before marriage and, though less since then, saw themselves at affectionate people. They were verbal and expressive and in calmer moments they recognised that they both contributed to the difficulties. There was mutual criticism, defensiveness and at times stonewalling, but contempt, the most noxious of the four bad outcome predictors was not present. As Gottman (1999) noted, couples have both soluble and perpetual problems. Soluble problems find practical resolution and perpetual ones can be managed in more constructive ways.

In the PLISSIT model, Ray and Polly spent energy and time in Permission and Limited Information, individually and jointly. With Polly this included making sure I understood her cultural background and that she was comfortable with discussing sex. It was helpful being of similar ages. She had passed menopause and this was not an issue. She had not discussed sex before in any detail with anyone and held the assumption that if two people married then good sex would naturally evolve. With her first husband most of her sexual experience had been quite traditional. She had had two children without major difficulty. Sexuality had not been the cause of the failure of that relationship. The idea that a good sexual relationship was one that could be built through understanding one's self and one's partner, overcoming past hurts, and learning to communicate was novel to her. Over time, she read the King (1998) book but was not a prolific reader as English was a second language, and she was still employed. Later in therapy I recommended she read the short Weiner-Davis (2003) article in the hope that she would find permission and a way to feel empowered and maybe in Schnarch's (1997) terms some individuation, by taking some positive, unilateral initiative in breaking the sexual stalemate with Ray. We also worked over several months on the idea of buying and using a vibrator to help kick-start sexual arousal both for her and for Ray. In time she was able accept this proposal and experiment with it. In building up to this, the use of the vibrator and its purchase was also discussed in joint sessions. Ray was already comfortable with the idea since he had used one with former partners. Ray had previously attempted to use Viagra and would later try Cialis, which worked for him. Polly, however, was not comfortable with chemical solutions to their problem. She wanted his arousal to be more romantic. In the long run Ray was able to masturbate and increase his use of fantasy and other sexual aides, but for him this was second best and a waste given that he was married. He challenged these beliefs and, to his satisfaction, regained erectile function. I also suggested Schnarch's (2002) *Resurrecting Sex* in which he addressed issues of older couples with health and performance problems. Information about sex and relationships was avidly consumed by Ray, but it was necessary for me to relay essential aspects to Polly in session and to contain his temptation to lecture Polly (and his impatience for change!).

In the specific suggestions and intensive therapy parts of the PLISSIT model, organising the material into the Bernal and Baker categories rather than a chronological account is helpful. Treatment proceeded, weaving its way between dealing with their individual, interactional, relationship and contextual issues. As individuals over the course of therapy, both Polly and Ray had past and present health issues, and past marital trauma and psychological difficulties. Polly had suffered chronic migraines throughout her marriage as well as during the eight years she had been single in between them. They had no known cause and were unresolved by successive medical treatments. She suffered from insomnia and often wrote long emails to me and to Ray during the early hours of the morning. Antidepressant medication did not help. This eliminated one possible source of loss of libido. She was interested in the relaxation exercises I suggested, but this did not assist as the main issues were relational. She seemed to have been well out of her first marriage when she met and then married Ray. Although she had suffered domestic violence she did not exhibit symptoms she could relate to it. As Polly had passed menopause I checked with her to see if a vaginal estrogen cream would help her with desire and with arousal during intercourse (Berman & Berman, 2001). During the therapy she had a hysterectomy and recovered well from this.

On his side, Ray had a series of health issues that he was diligent in addressing with the help of his doctors. He had had a motorbike accident when he was young, but with cooperative partners happy to use the female superior position and a vibrator had found good sexual adaptation. The more recent car accident had resulted in surgery and a prolonged recovery. He had Peyroni's disease, with his penis having a lean to the right, but though this can be associated with erectile problems, it had not been problematic. He suffered chronic pain and self-medicated with alcohol, with detrimental consequences for the relationship. All this led to relationship issues. His drinking led to conflict since many of their fights occurred when he was intoxicated. Polly believed that if Ray loved her, he would not drink. He knew that his drunken behaviour upset her and was the occasion of much conflict. Once he had improved pain management, it was possible to gently educate him on the negative effects of alcohol marital harmony and erectile functioning. This was a long and difficult process. Additional medical counter-indications increased Ray's motivation to reduce his drinking. Polly was pleased with this shift.

In sessions we addressed their pattern of communication. Both were poor listeners and both had long lists of complaints. It was not easy to get them to focus on one topic at a time. I spent a lot of time making sure each of them felt their feelings, both surface and deeper ones, as well as ensuring their needs were understood by me in the hope of bridging the gap between them (Shaddock, 2000). They progressed some way to using time out, not withdrawing from each other, and resuming discussions at a later calmer time (Stuart, 1980). Ray tended to pursue and Polly to withdraw, bringing unresolved matters into session (King, 1998). This pattern was highlighted and, though they still succumbed to it, they each understood their part in the dance and the possible steps they could take to moderate or manage it.

Polly, a light-sleeper, was disturbed by Ray's loud snoring. Both had sleep difficulties, which contributed to their low mood and irritability with each other. I discovered this after asking them to record Ray's snoring — it was very loud. The best adaptation they had found was for her to go to bed earlier so that she would be sound asleep when he came to bed. They did try it for a few nights in an attempt to see the effect on Polly's migraines, depression and general wellbeing. Sleeping in separate rooms was not a viable solution because Ray associated the meaning of marriage with the shared matrimonial bed. Trust was a sensitive area given their respective abandonment and financial abuse by previous partners. Any perceived gesture of pulling away became a threat, even actions designed to improve the quality of their interaction. The sense of abandonment for Ray and Polly's need to be caring would overwhelm the intentions to see the effect on their sexual relationship. Eventually, Ray attended a sleep clinic. He tried a continuous positive airway pressure (CPAP) machine, but relinquished it at Polly's initial innocent comment that it looked funny and that it too was noisy. Eventually, he found the Buteyko breathing therapy through a physiotherapist. This required disciplined daily practice and helped diminish his snoring, with the added bonus that he felt better and was able to lose weight. Unfortunately, other health issues and visitors would periodically disrupt the privacy of his regular breathing practice.

Tracking interaction through the sleep difficulties helped me realise that there was a major relationship rule operating. Both Ray and Polly much preferred to be givers rather than receivers. They were very generous with each other financially and poured respective resources into the common pot. Polly was a tremendous cook who enjoyed preparing exotic dishes for Ray. He in turn drove her everywhere and kept a garden they were proud of. They enjoyed giving, but if the balance between them looked unequal their old fear of being used would emerge. They were also reactive to situations in which the other might seem bossy or controlling. For each of them it was difficult to adhere to any seemingly 'selfish' strategy. Thus, Polly gave up separate sleeping arrangements and Ray, the CPAP machine as soon as the slightest objection was raised. This pattern was most likely entrenched in their respective personalities long before they met in their families of origin as well as their first marriages. Being the giver was a measure of self-esteem and being needed was a sign of being esteemed. We attempted to address their need to differentiate and self-soothe on this front as well as on others (Schnarch, 1999). They often took any comment from the other as a personal slight. The vulnerability they perceived in each other would compound this still further. On the rare occasions they did get close to intercourse one would easily give up for fear of pushing the other too far. Ray feared stressing Polly, and Polly feared making all his physical problems worse. Schnarch (1997, 2002) described the fear and vulnerability older couples face in the shadow of the possible death of a partner. Increasing intimacy, sexual and emotional, only adds to their fear of loss of the other. Polly's behaviour seemed to reflect this and she said that she did not want to matters worse for Ray. During one near sexual encounter he developed an acute urinary tract infection needing hospitalisation. We had carefully planned for possible obstacles to intercourse, predicting, for example, how they would cope if Ray got a erection but it did not last, how they would work together to renew it, how they would cope if Polly got the giggles and not be overcome by embarrassment or distraction. Fate intervened in a most unfair way with further illness for Ray and discouragement for both of them.

Several times during therapy there were interruptions to our process due to surgery for each of them. Typically, during postoperative recovery when all sexual expectations were on hold, their relationship was harmonious. They proved dedicated and appreciative partners during phases requiring carer-and-patient teamwork. Then they were restrained by circumstances from role conflict and competing to be the best giver but were able to settle into comfortable complementarity.

Relational dynamics of togetherness and separateness (Hendrix, 1988) or lack of differentiation (Schnarch, 1997) also played out in their social and family relationships. At the start of therapy Ray had given up visiting a friend during the day while Polly was at work. He saw Polly as being controlling but acquiesced to her perceived request to stop seeing his friend in order to preserve their relationship. In fact, she objected to their drinking together, but not to Ray seeking company during the day. She, in turn, had forsaken trips alone to the mall to shop and coffees with friends for similar reasons. It seemed to Ray that this need of hers covered a rejection of his company. Each were able to work though this pattern, be more comfortable and self-soothing of fears of rejection or abandonment, as well as to become more involved in separate activities once the meaning of time to oneself or with same-sex friends was clarified. They had two other couples as friends, one from each of their cultural backgrounds. They were both immensely fond of the couple from hers and operated like family with them. With the Western couple, moments of jealousy and exclusion would arise but would not last.

Interestingly, late in our therapeutic contact, they revealed to me that in fact they had managed before marriage on a very few occasions with the assistance of Viagra to have full intercourse. They seemed to have forgotten about it and maybe with all our work had overcome the shame and or cultural taboos of revealing premarital sexual activities to me. This seemed to be a surprising but hopeful sign.

Our work together did not achieve a regular pattern of satisfactory intercourse. However, there were significant gains. They had access to better information about sexuality. The meanings attributed to each other's behaviour and the associated feelings were softer and more complex thanks to gains in mutual understanding. They still fought. On the whole they had managed to survive these with less damage to their individual functioning and self-esteem. They were able to be more affectionate. Polly enjoyed receiving Ray's generous back rubs while lying on the couch watching TV together. I hope they get the occasional better night's sleep, with one of them in the in the spare room or together, when he is using his breathing exercises. Ray handled his drinking better. Polly mentioned this repeatedly as a positive outcome. They each have resumed the right to some separate activities. With aging and Ray's numerous health problems, Polly in particular has accepted that a full sexual relationship may not be possible. I anticipate that more grieving for this will occur for them. On the other hand, I hope they have developed more varied and frequent 'outercourse' practices, including possibly the use of the vibrator (King, 1998). Ray found that he rediscovered his erectile potential though the re-sexualisation program with another sex therapist, and this was tremendously encouraging. He felt he had regained his identity as a male deserving of Polly as a very attractive female. They had the potential to develop a more harmonious companionship and enjoy their activities and holidays together.

I thank both of them for all they taught me in the time we spent working in therapy. At the time of writing, I rang them and am delighted to know that they are together and, as far as I could tell, sounded happy. Polly often feared that their sessions in which they each felt understood with me were what kept them together. It would appear that they achieved independent competence of a lasting nature. I express my appreciation for their permission to present this abbreviated illustration of their therapeutic journey to illustrate the complexity of sex therapy.

I now propose two tentative outlines of what I hope might become a baseline for training for clinical psychologists working in sex therapy. First is a list of the areas of knowledge useful to clinicians:

- basic clinical training including cognitive–behavioural therapy (CBT) and mindfulness or acceptance and commitment therapy (ACT)
- couple therapy, various approaches
- systems theory and therapy
- sexual education, sexual health including medical/pharmacological knowledge of sexuality
- sex therapy
- knowledge of sexual practices and sexual aids
- communications skills, assertiveness, negotiation
- trauma therapy
- awareness of gender issues, religious/cultural/racial values
- community resources/other professionals in area of practice.

Second, I put forward a list of the desirable attitudes and qualities for clinical psychologists practicing as sex therapists:

- comfortable with own sexuality and with self
- clear boundaries and ethical standards

- comfortable discussing sex with others
- awareness of own values/respect for other's values
- comfortable with variations of sexual preference
- empathy
- good therapeutic and teaching skills
- up-to-date knowledge
- experience in intimate relationships
- flexibility and creativity
- have a model/a plan/a process
- positive attitude and ability to engender hope.
- multidisciplinary approach: doctor + specialists/allied health professionals + sex therapist
- regular supervision and professional development.

Chapter 8

When personality disorder adds to relationship problems

Who can draw a square circle? This Zen-like task evokes the seeming impossibility of working with difficult couples.

Any disorder of personality will affect intimate relationships. Carefully crafted images soon crumble in a context of intimacy. Predictable themes emerge that affect counselling, including an illusion of being special, problems distinguishing fantasy from reality, extremes of emotional deadness or intense chaotic feelings, messy communication, an aloof arrogance or insatiable need. If either partner suffers a psychological injury, then the result may be vicious retaliation. It is about chaotic worlds — without and within.

Perhaps nothing is more challenging than couple therapy when communication is distorted and there is little or no capacity for self-focus. Emotions explode in the 'safe place' of therapy. Is it possible to deal with such 'borderline states' in a therapeutic way without separating the couple and returning to safer territory? Sophisticated models of personality are needed to work with such couples, followed by 'fine tuning' techniques in order to be more effective.

As much as I value the contribution of Gottman, he was not enthusiastic about addressing issues characteristic of personality disorder. He noted that one of the problems with diagnostic labels is that the label does not automatically suggest something you can do (Gottman, 1999, p. 266). He preferred to talk in terms of what attachment theorists call an 'internal working model' and he mentioned Pinsof and Wynne's (1995) point that the mode of therapy should be based not so much on symptoms initially presented but on the nature of the resistance the therapist encounters. Gottman said that resistance due to individual psychopathology is seen in two ways: (1) psychopathology renders the uninfluenced steady state highly negative in the first place and adds bias to how neutral actions are seen (e.g., abuse sees things as controlling, depression leads to pessimism about interactions and paranoia can lead to jealousy); and (2) psychopathology distorts the way a person influences and accepts influence. It can mitigate against 'we-ness' and cohesion in a relationship (e.g., antisocial, narcissistic with entitlement, borderline, and drug and alcohol dependence). However, he added that there is a lot of relationship pathology that is not based on individual pathology. He also acknowledged that the biggest challenge for therapies is dealing with specific issues and comorbid psychopathologies, and this would include marital work with depression, alcohol, previous violence, an affair, previous abuse history or traumas, sexual problems and chronic physical illness (Gottman, 1999, p. 306). Emotion-focused couple therapy (EFT-C) has interesting ideas that could perhaps be more directly applied to working with personality related issues — for example, the relationship between shame and narcissistic vulnerability (Greenberg & Goldman, 2008, p. 322); however, in general it has not been well developed.

I would like to offer the following model, largely drawn from psychoanalytic theory, to understand the dynamics of personality disorder and potentially contribute to case formulation.

A portrait of the primitive self

Kohut and Kernberg agreed on very little in the debates that raged in psychoanalysis in the later half of the 20th century. Both described the primitive or immature self as a *grandiose self*.[3] Essentially Kohut (1971) saw the difficulty in terms of arrested development. What is perfectly natural for an infant is dysfunctional in an adult. Kernberg (1986) conceived of this self in terms of more ingrained psychopathology defended by primitive defences. The self is deeply flawed with 'a pathological self-structure'. His formulation of the problem was different — as was his cure!

It is possible to conceive of a *primitive self* underlying all of the personality disorders, and not just the narcissistic in terms of a grandiose self, which might be used interchangeably, though distinguished by different clusters of dominant traits. The following are characteristic:

- *Omnipotence.* The primitive self is essentially grandiose and omnipotent. This can lead to a denial of reality. The quality of omnipotence is often experienced by a partner as highly controlling. The 'tyrant' will punish any act of autonomy! The illusion of self-sufficiency must be preserved at all costs.

- *Flawed emotional regulation.* Such a self is emotionally immature and vulnerable to 'borderline states'. This is obvious in poor frustration tolerance, impulsive acts, and emotional tantrums. McCormack (2000) described 'using words not for communication but as projectiles' (p. 39). Anger is hard to contain, with rages that lead to emotional or physical abuse. A lack of self-soothing structures can lead to an overwhelming urgency of demand. Needs are 'all or nothing'. Because of a poor sense of constancy, any absences of the partner are frightening, stimulating fears of abandonment, and resulting in escalating demands. Naturally this can result in over-dependence in the relationship.

- *Hypersensitivity.* The primitive self is anything but robust. Normal disappointments, disapproval from the partner or others, and even attempts at helpful criticism can be devastating. Almost everything hurts. Everything offends. It is always felt as a personal attack. Kohut (1971) wrote about a vulnerability to 'narcissistic injury' (p. 10). In relationships there may be an expectation of exquisite sensitivity from others, with 'returns' of brutal retaliation if personal needs are not met.

Relationships are intensely reactive and often fester with a barely masked rage.

- *Unaware of self.* This includes a relative absence of an observing ego and any genuine insight. One aspect is identity diffusion. What is missing is a coherent sense of the self across time and in differing circumstances. Pervasive fragmentation leads to a lack of internal integration. This self reacts and is not reflective. The past is not really past, with enactment being an unconscious means of remembering. The profound lack of self-awareness relates to the use of defense mechanisms that deny or distort reality especially in relation to the self. This lack of insight can be intensely frustrating for the treating psychologist.

- *Unaware of people.* Others are seen globally in terms of needs and fears. Relationships are not so much a healthy 'I-You' but 'I-It' (Buber, 1937, 2004) or 'I-I' (Scott Peck, 2002). At the most primitive level the other is nothing more than an extension of the self. This results in difficulties with empathy. Defences such as projection also add to the interpersonal distortion and make it difficult to find a way forward in couple therapy. The combination of being unaware of self and other means that there is little agreed reality for the couple or therapist.

- *Idiosyncratic interpretations of reality.* Essentially this is the result of transference. Past and present are emotionally confused. Meaning is located in that highly charged inner world, and what follows is an impenetrable certainty and misplaced dogmatism. The internal image is well known but confused with the external person. This goes some way towards explaining what is familiar in couple therapy: a couple can describe an event accurately, but interpret it oddly (McCormack, 2000, p. 35). Reality is reduced to ever simpler categories; indeed it is 'morphed' to fit. This puts enormous pressure on an intimate partner. One of my students referred to this in vivid terms as the narcissist 'colonising the minds' of others.

- *Polarised relationships.* The primitive self has a tendency either to merge or be detached in relationships. Potentially nurturing others are not experienced as stable or reliable, and the result is either to escalate demands towards fusion or retreat into a state of schizoid pessimism about needs ever being met. The partner may experience this as irrational entitlement and feel 'used'. The primitive desire is for either merger or murder — thus 'co-mangling relationships' (McCormack, 2000, p. 159).

It is important to distinguish between *visiting* such states, which is what most people under acute stress will do from time to time in an intimate relationship, and *remaining* there most of the time — a characteristic of personality disorder.

> Michael was a partner at an international accountancy firm. He had a reputation for being irritable and demanding. Junior staff often felt bullied. He met Amanda through an escort service. Eventually the relationship with her changed from customer and sex worker, but never became stable. The constant state of crisis was exacerbated when Amanda fell pregnant. Michael left his wife of over 15 years because 'she never gave me a kid'. Amanda was ambivalent about remaining pregnant and having a baby. Michael also had some concerns about Amanda's dependence on alcohol and how this might affect the healthy development of the child.
>
> Michael and Amanda were passionate in every sense of the word. Anger flared quickly and tears followed. Sessions were intense. The problem, therapeutically, was to keep a sense of focus. Both tended to fly from topic to topic, emotionally dumping and resolving nothing.

The challenge of couple therapy

With clear borderline traits Amanda showed her primitive self with an overflow of unprocessed emotion. Her needs were over-whelming. Michael displayed his grandiosity as a sense of being entitled. He *had* to be in control.

As the treating psychologist, I found the sessions frustrating and agonising. In the face of excessive aggression and hostility I was left feeling bruised and violated. And at a trivial level I was worried about the noise in sessions carrying to other offices.

The sessions had the quality of an 'emotional psychosis'. Nothing became clearer. Issues that should be simple and straightforward were confused by self-absorption, extremes of emotional reaction, highly personalised conclusions and responses enflamed by narcissistic vulnerability. It was easy to see the influence of personality disorder with underlying problems in self-soothing, over-dependence and a pervasive terror of abandonment.

An initial practical problem is counter-transference. My first reaction is an urgency to leave the room or refer (get rid of!) the patients. Often at the end of a session I felt a resentment about how much emotional energy the session has cost me in the counselling process. I was tempted to heighten the 'us-them' divide with labels (e.g., narcissistic, borderline, psychopath). While there is some value in diagnosis, at this point such labelling is more a survival mechanism. I often feel inadequate. Perhaps the hardest struggle is with what is mostly unconscious, including fragments of infantile states such as feeling persecuted, hated, deprived, abandoned, unloved and neglected. There is a revival of feelings long ago disavowed and, until this kind of therapy, successfully buried (McCormack, 2000, p. 9).

It is stating the obvious that the first priority is to attempt to contain the emotionality and create a greater sense of psychological safety — for couple and therapist.

The couple will tend to focus on concrete behaviours — usually with endless complaints about the partner. Often there is an expectation of instant results, and while this is mostly impossible, it is perhaps reasonable to receive something helpful in the first session. The pull in early sessions is to respond to endless emergencies. By attempting to address such crises, the couple will feel that the therapist is responsive to their concerns. Naturally, unconscious themes are present in abundance. The primitive self has its own attraction for psychoanalytic therapy, but such a direct focus on the deeper levels may assume time not initially available.

Usually issues 'spill onto the table' and the therapist will quickly gain a sense of dysfunctional interaction. This will happen quite spontaneously, although a quieter partner may need to be drawn out and their share of the time balanced. When the interaction is largely hostile with little or no capacity for self-focus, the therapeutic process can become costly by eroding what little goodwill remains in the relationship. Emotional abuse and perhaps episodes of violence can be part of the picture. Safety is enhanced, but never guaranteed, by boundaries, boundaries and more boundaries.

It is essential for the psychologist to be highly directive and abundantly clear in what behaviour in a session is allowed and what is not tolerated. For example, tell both people to listen and not interrupt, arrive for the session on time and in a fit state to do therapy, and that you will allow no abusive or aggressive behaviour.

> Amanda came to the second session intoxicated and this was challenged. Michael when enraged would call Amanda 'the f-ing bitch'. This was confronted.

> In the third session the anger was so intense that I thought it best to separate them and saw them individually for about 10 minutes each.

Writing down the 'rules of engagement' is even more concrete, and once agreed, both can sign a therapeutic contract. This can give a precedent for later agreements. If possible, create an island of safety in what has become an unsafe relationship.

Of course, thinking about personality disorder physical safety should not be neglected. Gottman (1999) noted that highly anti-social men are not only violent to their partners but also to co-workers, family and strangers. Aggression in this case seemed trait related. While he acknowledged that some couples will present with extremes of personality disorder and psychopathology, 'in general it adds very little' (Gottman, 1999, p. 20, also pp. 118, 128–129). I disagree and believe that traits of personality is a challenge to find tougher interventions for difficult relationships.

Sometimes it helps to focus on some common issues. In a spirit of fairness 'list three issues each'. Some couples, with little sense of self or each other, are often very unclear about relationship issues, tending to make unending complaints, so making these three issues concrete can provide some focus. In addition to isolating points of contention and creating some space around the issues, the couple can be helped to deal with hot issues in a more productive way. This will give a different sense of what is possible in the relationship, and some progress will help restore a measure of hope and lessen the grip of despair. The couple will also get a sense of the psychologist and whether he or she is strong enough to handle them.

It is possible to adapt EFT-C to working with traits of personality disorder. The focus is the same, working to distinguish primary and secondary emotions in the 'here and now' of couple interactions. The containing function of the psychologist is very important: 'tolerate no nonsense' and strongly advocate for the relationship in spite of the manifold ways of the couple to sabotage therapeutic progress. Greenberg and Goldman (2008) noted that some people lack the ability to self-soothe because they lack internal emotional structures and have difficulty holding onto even the good things in the present relationship. He suggested identifying where in the body the feeling is, breathing into that place (in a mindful way), naming the deep vulnerability 'I feel like I can't survive this', 'I am disappearing', 'I am bad, disgusting', and through this symbolising process beginning to get a handle on the feeling. This naming creates some distance and there is an opportunity for perspective. This can lead to an effort to change the mood perhaps through a favourite activity. It can also be helpful to think back to a time when the relationship was good and try to believe that it can be again in the future — using the image or memory to self-soothe. It is helpful to counter the feeling, say invalidation, with the thought of a time in the relationship in which there was a sense of being affirmed. And finally 'they need to connect with their own internal resources and literally be able to soothe themselves by imaging themselves being compassionate and validating and taking care of the vulnerable part of themselves' (Greenberg & Goldman, 2008, pp. 164–165).

A useful intervention, also recommended by Greenberg and Goldman (2008), at times of emotional dys-regulation is to ask the person to imagine a child who feels the same feelings as they are feeling, sitting in the chair in front of them, a child who has suffered as they have suffered and then: 'What would you say to that child who felt those feelings?' and What would you feel towards that child?' Typically this will evoke compassion and the recognition of what the child (and self!) need. Then imagine responding to the child within, in a similar way. Starting with a universal child may help to side-step feelings of self-contempt.

It is possible to work simultaneously on two levels: surface and depth. The surface issues are obvious. What is less obvious is the process of strengthening of the treatment alliance. There is the necessity of being a strong container to hold the emotional reactivity both will bring to sessions. In this instance containment is not only for the individuals but the relationship. The treating psychologist will also be a target for transference dynamics, which can help us to better appreciate early childhood experiences that are now experienced in vivo.

While the psychologist may be working in a very concrete way in the early sessions, theory is still important. One of the more common complementary patterns in this work involves borderline and schizoid spouses. This is an expression of the polarised relationship of two primitive selves. The schizoid spouse expects the rejection of needs, hurt and humiliation, and the escalation of aggression. The risk of feeling need in any form is to recapitulate childhood experiences when it was unsafe to have normal needs. This kind of person will value rationality, absolute self-control, and use emotional withdrawal. Naturally this will be intensely frustrating for the partner, who will be provoked into even greater extremes of emotional reactivity (McCormack, 1989, pp. 299–309). The creation of a climate of safety is essential for the schizoid spouse because he or she will hope that eventually needs may be recognised and responded to in better ways. The borderline spouse also needs safety and reassurance, but because this person is so expressive the therapist can easily see the disjunction and respond appropriately.

Once some sense of safety is established in sessions, the psychologist may try to establish times of emotional connection in the couple relationship. Traditional techniques are helpful, such as anger scales with strategies to break well before the danger zone, use of 'I-language', attentive listening, strategies for conflict resolution and safe places. David Schnarch recommended techniques like 'hugging till relaxed' (Schnarch, 1997, pp. 157–186).

It is important for the psychologist to adopt an empathic stance. I try to commit myself to understanding each person's experience of difficulties in the relationship from the inside rather than try unrealistically to be an 'objective' observer. This takes continual effort because the couple will appeal to you as a 'justice of the family court'. When successful the empathic stance is 'experience near'.

The next step is separation and more healthy connection.

In the case example, Michael wanted Amanda to be more responsible in terms of self-care and Amanda wanted emotional support from Michael. On the surface these two issues are distinct, seem reasonable and negotiation should be possible, but with the complexity of their relationship it was important to disentangle:

- overwhelming feelings of rejection at the slightest hint of withdrawal
- exaggerated feelings of intrusion and unreasonable demands that can come from ghosts of previous relationships or unresolved issues of conflict
- controlling or bullying patterns of behaviour
- lack of being able to hold on to any reassurance of love
- need related explosions of anger
- elaborate self-justification with absolute moral certainty
- emotional addiction to crisis.

The advantage of an emotional focus is that it is always experienced by the couple as relevant to their concerns and progress is 'felt' rather than judged.

The themes listed earlier indicate the intrusion and distortion of primitive self-states. This step features repeated clarification: (a) Amanda needed to appreciate that when she experienced Michael's withdrawal it was not necessarily a personal rejection; (b) his irritability could be the result of work issues and did not signal unhappiness about the relationship; (c) when he worked late, she may experience feelings of abandonment, but it did not mean that he was having an affair; (d) Michael was too controlling and in part this related to his exaggerated sense of responsibility in the relationship. He did not believe that Amanda could care for herself, and while there were grounds for his concern, she had a history of functioning in many areas of her life without his obsessive monitoring.

Expectations can usually be addressed with better functioning couples, but with Amanda and Michael it was almost impossible to 'reality test' what is a reasonable or an unreasonable request. And yet it is an important topic in sessions because it can help self and other clarification regardless of how 'muddy the water is'.

We can help to enhance honest feedback. Naturally this is not always positive. This includes an opportunity to learn more healthy patterns of assertiveness. Shaddock (2000) recommended a policy of 'touch and go', in which a person will comment briefly enough to register a negative reaction, 'I really dislike it when you are sarcastic' or 'You seem irritable'. But it is helpful to stop then and avoid the ruts of familiar arguments.

When there is a question of remaining in the relationship, it can be helpful to clarify a 'bottom line'. This is essential with overpowering issues like violence, substance abuse or affairs.

The work of careful clarifying of differences will eventually lead to more insight.

> Amanda described the shift from a more narcissistic perspective in a relationship: she moved from immediately jumping to the conclusion 'He doesn't enjoy me anymore' to the recognition 'He is depressed'.

Often need is about connection. Unfortunately the level of demand can be overwhelming and often one partner will withdraw. But this is more turbulent than the familiar pursuer and distancer pattern in most relationships. Unmet need will fuel conflict and generate tantrum-like behaviour. Rather than maintain the 'stand-off' it is preferable to find more satisfying ways of connecting. I will try to negotiate 'anchor places' for the relationship in which both can attempt to be emotionally present.

> Michael and Amanda agreed to arrange a sitter and have a meal out once a week. It was agreed to avoid all hot topics. While the intention was there, both had busy schedules and this was sometimes missed. They would sometimes fall into conflict, but nevertheless it did begin to provide more positive interactions and an occasional sense of connection.

Caring days and caring behaviours can provide some positive experiences (see Hendrix, 1988). Naturally all of this is difficult with people, who with the fragility of the primitive self, will tend to focus on survival rather than emotional fulfilment.

Communication is always difficult. While it is impossible not to communicate something in a couple relationship, dysfunctional patterns will tend to sabotage healthy connection. The principles of Gottman (1999) are relevant here but frankly even harder to put into practice. Indeed, when working with such couples I notice a subterranean quality that indicates that most of what is important remains unsaid or is clouded by trivia. Unconscious dynamics intrude and this places the source of problems beyond the awareness of everyone, including the therapist. Again it is helpful to think in terms of what is 'needed' by the primitive self — which may not be intelligible except within this theoretical context.

While the therapist can model empathy it is more of a challenge to encourage it in the interactions of the couple. I have found it helpful to work with couples with exercises; however hard it is, sometimes this can provide a different model of interaction. It can give a measure of hope. Unfortunately, it is almost impossible for difficult couples to put it into practice outside of the therapeutic context. In all this there is an opportunity to work at a deeper level. The empathy of the therapist, exploring the subjective experience of each person, will give a taste of more optimal interpersonal responsiveness — what Kohut (1971) called a self-object. Sometimes it is helpful to ask a person to imaginatively put themselves into the experience of the other. How does the partner feel? Think about an issue? See the future? Then the partner can clarify their own experience in terms of what has been said. Sometimes a couple will find an exercise such as role reversal helpful. The primitive self is often 'mirror hungry' and positive experiences of empathy, especially from the partner, will give energy to the relationship.

Another important dimension is mutual understanding. The therapeutic process encourages self-insight and a better appreciation of couple dynamics. It is helpful to explore such areas as families of origin, childhood relationships with parents, and previous patterns in intimate relationships. There is a place for bibliotherapy, reading relevant books, and perhaps encouraging the couple to maintain a journal of the relationship. Individual therapy can also assist, perhaps with another therapist (Shaddock, 2000, pp. 127–139).

> Amanda found sessions with dialectical behaviour therapy very helpful in trying to self-regulate her variable moods.

Indeed, anything that assists emotional self-regulation (e.g., acceptance and commitment therapy, mindfulness-based CBT, or dialetical behaviour therapy [DBT]) is enormously helpful. The obvious advantage of looking at 'my stuff' in a relationship is that it is an area under personal control and change is possible.

It is of course not possible to 'instantly' develop an observing ego. One suggestion is to listen for a wisdom figure from a person's family of origin or past experience.

> Michael had an abusive mother, and a father who failed to protect him. He had only one positive figure, his paternal grandmother, and at times he would spend weeks with her.

This person can then be gradually incorporated into the process of therapy. Questions could then be asked, such as: 'What would your grandmother think about this?', 'What would she have said?', and 'How would you feel having her support?' Such a wisdom figure can provide an intermediate step along the way of developing that observing part of the self that can add objectivity, contain overflowing feelings, and even soothe the self with positive self-talk.

Stereotyped roles, such as *persecutor*, *victim* and *rescuer*, can be recognised and better understood. Relationship patterns can become more obvious.

> Amanda noted that she would verbally abuse Michael until there was an open discussion of separation and then she would frantically try to hold on to him with acts of extravagant submission.

> Michael began to gain more insight into his rampant narcissism.

Some people who feel special will adopt denial as a defence and flee 'reality as the enemy'. The treating psychologist can help to support the patient while stripping away layers of illusion. It is helpful to recognise and self-critique the 'larger than life' narratives. Stephen Mitchell (1988) saw narcissism in terms of *offer* and *acceptance*. It is a two-way process in a couple relationship and such dynamics can be better understood.

Kohut (1971) used the term 'self-object' to refer to experiences of nurture such as being soothed, recognised or protected. Intimate adult relationships recreate childhood dynamics around self-object failure. This adds intensity to the couple interaction, especially around common themes of intrusion and abandonment. It can be helpful to explore such longings, using interpretation to normalise them (since dependency needs can evoke shame). In this way the relationship can be understood in terms of mutual regulation with repeated failures.

Some aspects of the primitive self appear to be linked to early trauma. McCormack (2000) noted: 'The mutual ground of borderline relationships is located in the unrelenting efforts of each spouse to master unresolved traumas of the past and resultant developmental deficits' (p. 18). Often an injured person will attempt to communicate the trauma with anger, exaggeration or acting out, which is commonly dismissed by the partner. It emerges in two stages in the relationship: (1) the emotional pain, and (2) the failure to be soothed by the caretaking other. Gradually the traumatised person will be able to better recognise the nature of the parental relationships that permitted such abuse, allowed the impact to go unrecognised and not amended. Locating the source of pain in the family-of-origin will help to take some heat off the partner.

The primitive self reacts; it does not reflect. The pathological nature of the inner world of object and self-representations becomes manifest through enactment. Reflection and timely interpretation can help the process of understanding. And it is very validating for a person, within the context of a primary relationship, to have the injury named and then emotionally repaired, initially by the therapist, but perhaps later repair can be encouraged in the relationship.

The odd thing is that even a sensitive and empathic partner can inadvertently navigate the relationship into troubled waters. The paradox is that sometimes a responsive partner will create a stable environment for the emergence of archaic longings — the intensity of which can be surprising. It can be helpful for the couple therapist to recognise this with a statement like, 'You have made the relationship safe enough for your partner to trust you with these needs' (Shaddock, 2000, p. 44.)

In the case of Amanda and Michael, the following incident provided the focus for the next session.

> Amanda was convinced that Michael had a 'one night stand' with a junior accountant in the firm. Michael vigorously denied the allegation and called Amanda 'paranoid'. This led to a confrontation on the previous weekend that included shouting and some pushing.

I carefully listened to the experience of both Amanda and Michael, attempting to slowly understand the various *meanings* of what happened. There had been enough therapeutic progress for Amanda and Michael to slow down, examine cues for emotional reactions, interrupt enactments and demonstrate that 'there can be room in a relationship for different realities'. (Shaddock, 2000, p. 93.)

It is helpful to distinguish present needs from past needs. Stolorow, Brandchaft, and Atwood (1995) underlined the importance of understanding 'organising principles' from infancy and childhood. The observation is made: 'Transference is neither a regression to nor an displacement from the past, but rather an expression of the *continuing influence* of organising principles and imagery that crystallised out of the patient's early formative experiences' (Stolorow et al., 1995, p. 36.) These principles become something like a black hole, assimilating present events into old meanings, and locking people into affect states and defensive behaviours. The challenge is help the couple understand how the past haunts the relationship on a daily basis.

Amanda felt betrayed when Michael lost interest in her sexually. It was just for a week or so and related to work pressure. She took it personally and gradually her anger built up to spill over in the next session.

The goal in the next session was to interrupt the rage and try to restore an empathic link. When understanding was re-established, I could begin to interpret the self-object longings. And I was able to point out that Amanda's rage triggered reactions in Michael that were the opposite of what was actually sought — nurture cannot usually be bullied out of a partner!

Sometimes it is helpful to frame interpretations in terms of the relationship rather than the individuals: 'There is a struggle in the relationship for more intimacy, but at times it is too much and the anger followed by withdrawal gives breathing spaces'. Thomas Ogden (1999) talked about the 'analytic third' created between therapist and client (pp. 459–492), a concept that is useful in couple therapy. This kind of externalising can enable a systems perspective and has the advantage of being less blaming and better accepted by the couple.

And finally, growth. Personality disorder is fundamentally a disorder of the self, so the challenge will always be to facilitate emotional maturity and deal with pathological self-structures. This kind of change is more likely to happen at an unconscious level with the primitive self, but will include a better regulation of self and affect states in the relationship.

Amanda was able to learn to use mindfulness techniques to calm herself and not make the urgent demands on Michael, while he saw his withdrawal to over-focus on work as an unhelpful strategy for coping.

Dysfunctional relationships tend to be 'lean to' or utilitarian. The challenge is to help a couple move towards self-reliance and healthy mutuality. When the intensity of demand decreases, the partner will be less of a resource and more of a companion. It is exciting to see the emergence of a new space for symbolic activity, including 'thinking, play, creativity, metaphor, poetry, art, philosophy and spirituality' (McCormack, 2000, p. 159). Shaddock (2000) used the analogy of improvisation in jazz music to illustrate the balance of freedom and connection.

Couples with traits of personality disorder present in couple therapy. This is inevitable and the therapeutic process is fraught with difficulty, often ending with a sense of failure for the treating psychologist. Such therapy calls on a range of diagnostic and theoretical understanding that is emphasised in the training of clinical psychologists. It is important to have a developed theory of personality, informed by developmental research, as illustrated by psychoanalytic psychotherapy and in couple treatment EFT-C. At times there is a need for empathic attunement, dealing with escalating emotions, and teaching self-soothing skills. It is a therapeutic challenge that asks for more, not less, in terms of skills and training.

A relationship is like a block of marble with two sculptors. It is the choices — large and small — that create what can become a work of art or a hideous object best hidden away from sight. Naturally the couple will need to do most of the work. Our role is to bring out the artist in them and trust the creative process.

Domestic violence

It is important to routinely check if conflict has ever involved domestic violence: emotional, psychological abuse, physical intimidation or aggression and social isolation. Usually, but not always, it is the female partner who is the victim of abuse and, given the difference in most males' and females' physical size, it is the female who is more at risk (Barnish, 2004; Hamel, 2005). Treatment approaches are outlined for abusers and abused, separately and together. Clinicians who often see couples with violence issues are well advised to get additional training and supervision while doing this work. The expected outcome of this kind of treatment is modest in the opinion of the authors reviewed and this note of caution needs to be made clear to clients who seek help (Gottman and Jacobsen, 1988).

If there is the risk of violence it is important to enquire about the severity of the risk. Barnish (2004) and Heru (2007) list the risk factors: a previous history of violent partner behaviour, uncontrolled continuous use of drugs or alcohol, fear of serious injury from the partner, past violence that required medical treatment, previous use of or threat of use of a weapon, death threats, stalking or other obsessional behaviour, sadistic behaviour, a man's history of being in an abusive family as a child, narcissistic or inflated and fragile self-esteem, and patriarchal sense of entitlement. Gottman and Jacobsen (1998) differentiate perpetrators into three groups:

1. *Low risk abuse* (couples where there is rare and low risk abuse not requiring medical intervention).

2. *Cobras* (estimated as 20% of high-risk abusers, often with criminal, sadistic and antisocial characteristics, are deliberate and calculating in their violence and the men, with typically very low heart rate, have cold, controlled instances of violence).

3. *Pit Bulls* (estimated to be 80% of high-risk abusers, who have gradually elevated heart rates, are more insecure men but also dangerous).

Typically, those in a relationship with a Cobra are more afraid of their partners than those of Pit Bulls. Barnish (2004), in her excellent review of the literature, finds support for a general classification of this type.

Treatment outcomes studies are not generally optimistic but there are some approaches that seem promising (Barnish, 2004; Heru, 2007; Meichenbaum, 2007). The perspective is generally feminist, and consideration for the safety of abused partner is the very first priority, followed by an expectation that the abuser will take full responsibility for his violent behaviour. It is not uncommon that the abused partner has or will have involvement with the police and the legal system. The best treatment approaches in the United States often involve a combination of individual therapy for both partners, gender specific groups (often court mandated for the abusers), telephone support for the victim, couple therapy and, later, couples group therapy (Capaldi & Kim, 2007; Hamel, 2005; Meichenbaum, 2007; Stith, et al., 2004). Included is a focus on the violence, examining and challenging gender-related values, psycho-education about stress and anger, and learning self-control rather than other-controlled behaviour. Hamel distinguished between an individual's unequivocal control over their behaviour, some control over one's internal emotional states, and finally no control over the other's feelings or behaviour; and understanding the origin of a partner's values and behaviour, and developing and integrating alternative, more cooperative interaction patterns. To my knowledge this kind of comprehensive treatment approach is not widely available in Australia. A good knowledge of local agencies and key staff (including police, domestic violence crisis unit, refuges, legal aid, health facilities and practitioners, family court) and coordination between all services involved with a couple facilitates better outcomes (Meichenbaum, 2007). A careful explanation of the clinician's duty of care is highly recommended. Obtaining the relevant releases of information from both parties is essential for appropriate and timely liaison with other agencies. This can be a delicate process depending on the stage at which violence is revealed to the therapist (Bograd & Mederos, 1999).

Gottman and Jacobsen (1988) are very cautious about the merits of couple therapy where there is violence except for couples with low-level or family-only intimate violence and, as others would emphasise, voluntary participation (Bograd & Mederos, 2004; Johnson, 2006). There is considerable research currently being done in the area of screening for couples' suitability for couple therapy, including the development of an Intimate Justice Scale IJS (Jory, 2004; Meichenbaum, 2007). However, as Goldner (1998) noted, couples often come for couple therapy where they would not approach any other type of treatment regardless of warnings about its limitations, and clinicians need to be prepared to offer a well-informed, skilled service as far as this is possible. Goldner (1998) is known to point out to a couple that it is only by chance that the issue of violence is being addressed in a counselling setting rather than a legal one. It is important to say that the focus of treatment is the violent behaviour. No matter what the explanation is for a perpetrator's violence, it is up to him to decide whether to abuse his partner or not. She distinguished between the batterer's responsibility for his violent behaviour and the responsibility of both for their relationship difficulties. She divided treatment into two phases: a consultation phase of 1 to 3 sessions in which the couple is evaluated as individuals in separate sessions and as a couple as to their readiness for therapy, followed by a therapy phase. The screening and assessment phase with separate sessions for each partner is crucial in determining the course of therapy. Bograd and Mederos (1999) outlined the essential information to be gathered at this stage:

- Is there violence?
- What is the nature, severity, frequency, duration and consequences of the violence?
- Provision of a detailed account of the aggression and its context.
- The function and impact of the violence.
- The degree of fear and felt intimidation by the abused.
- Is it part of a broader pattern of intimidation, domination, coercion, psychological and sexual abuse, abuse of children?
- Set the groundwork for an informed decision about the advisability of couple therapy or not. It is important to be aware

that men tend to minimise the degree of their violence and women may agree for fear of retribution.

The second phase is contingent on the male's ability to take full responsibility for his violent behaviour and show he can behave in other ways in situations where he used to erupt. Barnish (2004) emphasised, from her review of the literature, the importance of safety being emphasised and ensured as much as possible before couple therapy is undertaken. I say that any relapse into violent behaviour will totally undermine and render null any of the benefits of therapy.

Self-responsibility or agency-for-self is emphasised with men needing to take responsibility fully for their violence. Goldner (1998) emphasised the need for women to pay attention to the messages of their internal fear responses around their partners, no matter how sincere, romantic and hopeful partners' promises of ceased violence are. Some women who have lost their ability to think for or of themselves need coaching in how to develop or retrieve this aspect of self- agency. Heru (2007) and Hamel (2005) offered very useful check lists for women who feel unsafe and need to be prepared to separate and seek refuge:

- Memorise important and emergency phone numbers.
- Teach children these numbers and how to dial the local emergency number.
- Keep in a safe and private place information about help in domestic violence.
- Keep a mobile or change for a pay phone handy.
- If possible open a separate bank account.
- Set up support: friends, neighbours, family — and keep in touch.
- Rehearse the escape plan.
- Leave spare keys, money, clothes, copies of important identification, and documents (e.g., financial, health, insurance) with a trusted person.

• Know your rights, your legal situation, and where alternative accommodation can be found, including refuges in case staying with people known to the abuser is not desirable.

Heru (2007) also pointed out that for the women, assessment and treatment of depression and PTSD is also indicated, and for men, depression, drug and alcohol use, posttraumatic stress and personality disorders. While I will not cover this in detail, it is also important to pay attention to the security, health and psychological wellbeing of children in these families.

With men it is important to assess their violence: the degree, duration, prevalence (past, with animals, family, strangers), any neurological impairment, the meaning of the violence for the man, the history and severity of it with his current partner, his motivation to keep his marriage. Jenkins (1990), Goldner (1998), and Meichenbaum (2007) have noted that it is important to confront men with their violence without shaming them, but by helping them develop a sense of self-esteem connected to self-control, self-soothing of anger and frustration, and identification with respect for others.

Jenkins (1990) argued that men are restrained from treating partners with respect, sensitivity and consideration because of our society's patriarchal values and cultural norms stressing male supremacy, ownership, dominance and entitlement. He thought it was important to pit the man's motivation in opposition to the pull of this male ethos. Typical questions to a male client might be: 'What kind of relationship do you want to have with your partner? I need to understand what kind of marriage you want and what kind of marriage you have has in the past. Do you want a relationship where she lives in fear or do you want one where she can speak her mind and be fully with you, or do you want her to tiptoe around you? Do you want to be in charge of your relationship or do you want to follow these patriarchal notions? What kind of tests would you have to pass to prove to her that you were serious about leaving behind your violent behaviour?'

I recommend the following authors: Jenkins (1990), Hamel (2005), Goldner (1998) and Meichenbaum (2007).

Goldner (1998) conceptualised men's violence as both wilful, intentional, as well as emotional and impulsive. She posed confronting questions to abusers such as: 'What made you choose to lose it?' and 'Can you remember the moment when you chose to lose it?' She stated that it is important expand 'the man's self-description without negating his experience'. Men need to be coached and taught how to calm themselves, to hold back and to take time out, to leave the home if necessary, and to consider alternative action in circumstances in which there has previously been violence. Drawing up a list of steps (leave situation, walk around the block, breathe, call a friend, drink some water, remember conversations with therapist, invoke new ideas he wishes to adhere to, focus on emerging feelings and sensations of self-control, and so on) and alternatives, such as those for women, which would include crisis telephone support, emergency accommodation with friends, family or men's refuges. Working through with men their likely thoughts, actions, feelings and self-assessment along a new path, may add to their resolve and confidence to embark on this venture.

Goldner (1998) embarks on joint couple therapy only after a man has demonstrated that he can take full responsibility for his behaviour, shows remorse, understanding of and empathy for his partner's position and reactions, and is on a path of nonviolence for a few weeks (Gottman & Jacobsen [1998] would say six months). The other authors recommended above endorse this approach as well. Jenkins (1990) would reinforce by paying much attention to the abuser's new behaviour and victories over the old thinking patterns and reactions, as well as the meanings for his self-concept and beliefs.

Goldner (1998) would include getting to know both partners and their family-of-origin histories and patterns around conflict in the process of therapy. With both parties, she deconstructs violent biographies and moments. She attempts to articulate for the man where his actions in the present are linked with occasions in his past, how he is confusing his female partner with a previously abusive authority figure in his childhood, distinguishing past and present, and developing new and more constructive responses with his partner. For both partners it is important to examine the powerful force of attachment that has kept them together despite long years of unhappiness, conflict and fear, liberating it to evolve into more adaptive patterns.

In couple therapy, Jenkins would further emphasise the need for safety and responsibility. He would test out each person's readiness and ability to discuss and deal with previous areas of violence, severe conflict, differences, opinions, feelings and reactions. Jenkins said that 'Both are invited to externalise and challenges their restraints to the man accepting responsibility for his violence' (p. 104). For example, the woman, in accommodating, putting up with, forgiving, taking responsibility for his violence; and the man — does he still notice her taking this responsibility for him, or is he for himself? Does he think his partner can now speak up for herself and, if not, what could he do to convince her that he can handle her doing so? Jenkins recommended analysis of new interactions around old areas of disagreement in detail, the predictions of obstacles, set-backs and planning for dealing with them as they occur. He suggested setting realistic criteria for evaluating safety and success and warned against the woman prematurely trusting her male partner's change. Women, if unrealistically hopeful and trusting when their partners embark on a treatment program, may leave themselves more unprotected. And for the male, he must be wary of relaxing his guard on his attitude and old behaviour. Jenkins aimed to have partners take an equitable share of responsibility for the maintenance of the relationship and balance patterns of togetherness and independence in their lives together and to challenge the cultural pull of 'traditional' or patriarchal myths about male–female relationships.

It should be clear to all that any relapse of the male partner into violence at any stage of the therapeutic involvement — during the single-gender group phase, assessment, couple therapy or couples group phases — will lead to the involvement of police, legal intervention, as well as to the couple's permanent separation. Research indicates that the incidence of violent episodes is highly likely to increase during the six months after separation (Barnish, 2004). Care to involve both partners in individual separation counselling sessions is strongly encouraged at this stage, with paramount concern for the woman's safety. Couples' mediation within the context of the family court can be of use (Kelly & Johnson, 2006). Support groups for women can also be helpful. Liaison with other agencies and professionals is particularly indicated during this phase.

Chapter 9

Additional considerations: Different happy couples

Tolstoy in the famous first line to his novel *Anna Karenina* observed: 'Happy families are all alike; every unhappy family is unhappy in its own way'.

However, contrary to Tolstoy, there are a number of different ways that a couple can be happy. Gottman (1999) has distinguished three different relational styles. These are:

1. *Volatile couples*, in which each will immediately try to influence the other and such attempts will remain at a high level throughout the interaction. This couple is the most emotionally expressive. The whole range of emotions are expressed, including positive emotions such as humour, affection, interest, and teasing, as well as negative emotions such as anger and distress. This pair will have a working philosophy of being open with each other. There are high levels of disagreement as well as affection and humour. They tend to maintain an 'us versus the world' stance. Men in such relationships are as likely as the women to raise issues and tend not to stonewall. Both will stay committed to being romantic and re-wooing each other especially after damaging conflict. Both tend to see strength in the other and are supportive of mutual independence.

2. *Validating couples* attempt to influence the other, mainly in the middle of the conflictual interaction, less in the first-agenda building phase, and more in the later negotiation phase. There is a belief in emotional expressiveness, but in moderation, at

the right times and only on really important issues. There is great emphasis on 'we-ness' and companionship.

3. *Conflict-avoiding couples* never tackle conflict head-on. They will tend to quickly 'agree to disagree'. Both will minimise the importance of the problem, talk about the strengths in the relationship, reiterate their shared belief and value systems, reaffirm their commitment to each other, and then end the conversation on some note of solidarity or philosophical optimism (Gottman, 1999, pp. 88–89).

Gottman (1999) also acknowledges the difficulty of mismatches with couples and offers possible ways to deal with this. He has a model of 'sound marital house' with the following levels: foundation of friendship (creating positive affect in nonconflictual contexts), creating positive sentiment override, regulating conflict, and creating shared meaning. Each of these suggest various helpful interventions and couple exercises, which are included in his more popular *Seven Principles* (Gottman & Silver, 1999).

Two kinds of problems

Gottman (1999) distinguished two kinds of relationship problems: perpetual and solvable. In a four-year follow-up he found that even in happy marriages couples were still fighting about exactly the same things. Intractable issues make up 69% of the disputes. Most of the difficulties in a relationship never get resolved! So much for the power of communication.

These 'make-or-break' issues test the relationship but do not guarantee failure. Many couples come to an understanding that such difficulties are inevitable in the relationship:

> much the way that physical ailments are inevitable as you get older. They are like a trick knee, a bad back, an irritable bowel, or tennis elbow. We may not love these problems, but we are able to cope with them (Gottman & Silver, 1999, p. 131).

One psychologist said that choosing a long-term partner is to choose a particular set of unsolvable problems that the couple will grapple with for the next 10, 20 or 50 years (Wile, as cited in Gottman & Silver, 1999, p. 131). This sounds true to me after 38 years of marriage!

Some examples of perpetual problems:

• Nancy wants sex more often than Michael.

• Tom is more casual about having an ordered house than Amanda.

• Brett wants the children to be raised as Roman Catholic; his wife believes that this is submitting to human not divine authority.

• Kylie wants to pursue her career; Vince wants to begin a family by having children.

• Annie wants to go out and party; Brad wants to relax in front of the television.

• And an example from my own marriage — every election Jennie and I compete to influence the children with our own preference to vote Liberal or Labor.

In unstable relationships, perpetual problems tend to lower goodwill. Conversations cycle and remain stuck, with the couple becoming more frustrated and unhappy. It is all battle and no play. When either becomes emotionally disengaged, the end is in sight. All this is not necessary. But, first, consider solvable problems.

Solvable problems

Gottman (1999) suggested that difficulties in the solvable range seem less painful, gut-wrenching or intense. He argued that with solvable problems the focus of conflict is on the particular dilemma or situation. The issue is not loaded. There is no underlying conflict or difference in personality or values adding heat to the dispute. I am not sure it is this clear-cut, since some solvable problems can lead to conflict of great and lasting intensity.

Whether the problems are solvable or perpetual, it is essential to communicate acceptance of the other's personality. Mutual understanding is the best basis for making any changes in a relationship. Gottman and Silver sensibly added: 'In all arguments , both solvable and perpetual, no one is ever right. There is no absolute reality in marital conflict, only two subjective realities' (Gottman and Silver, 1999, p. 150). Most of the advice in marriage books, including a couple I have written, involves becoming a good listener and validating the other's perspective. Unfortunately, in the heat of the moment, it is very hard to do!

Gottman advises couples to (1) make sure that the start-up is soft, (2) learn to recognise and effectively use repair attempts, (3) monitor the self to avoid feeling flooded, (4) learn to compromise, and (5) become more tolerant of each other's imperfections. These are skills people generally use with friends, so it is just a matter of not forgetting them in the most intimate of relationships (Gottman & Silver, 1999, pp. 157–185).

Women tend to initiate by bringing up issues in relationships. While both males and females can be responsible for a harsh start-up, Gottman (1999) identified females as more often the catalyst. Also, remember that the end of a dispute usually has the same tone as the beginning. If conflict is to recover from initial harsh words, it will usually take a concerted effort. Gottman did not find much difference in the style of repair attempts between happy and unhappy couples, but he did notice that the repair attempts in happy relationships seemed to get through to the partner and were more effective. Often conflict will trigger flooding emotions in one or both of the couple, so this raises the need for self-soothing strategies. The psychologist can also help with this (e.g., breathing; progressive muscle relaxation; visualisation, including that of a safe place). If one person can become more relaxed, then they might be encouraged to help to soothe their partner, though naturally in the heat of a dispute this is very difficult — verging on impossible.

It is something of a cliché to assert that compromise is important in a happy relationship. If a relationship is dominated by one person's needs then it seems likely to be unstable, at least in our culture. Gottman (1999) argued that 'accepting influence' from the other is an important factor in establishing a compromise. Apparently men find it harder to accept influence and see a problem from the other's perspective. As a psychologist you can encourage the couple to both ask questions with open curiosity in order to see the issue from the other's perspective, and hopefully to establish some middle ground. Gottman recommended that each draw a large circle; inside the circle include issues about which compromise is possible; then draw an inner circle and only include 'no compromise' issues. This type of exercise can help the couple talk about issues and possibly find creative solutions to address core concerns. The compromise region will help to focus on what is possible. Of course, it is essential for the couple to be tolerant of the other's faults. In EFT-C the pattern of dominance and submission is addressed.

It should also be noted that any issue, no matter how trivial or seemingly easy to solve, may have a huge symbolic meaning that can be at the core of a person's sense of self. Such issues can easily become perpetual and gridlocked (Gottman, 1999, p. 220).

Perpetual problems
The goal is not to solve perpetual problems. What is important is for both to understand where their partner is coming from, to move away from being stuck in pain — what Gottman calls being gridlocked — and to begin to effectively dialogue about the differences.

The most common 'conflict zones' are predictable: work stress, in-laws, money, sex, housework, and raising children. These will also be issues in happy relationships. What is the 'work' of a marriage? (Couples so often cite the maxim that 'it takes work'.) Gottman said that it comes down to gaining a rich understanding of each other, especially in relation to difficult issues. It is helpful for both to feel safe and secure in the relationship. Additionally, there are very sensible, practical suggestions to dealing with such common relationship issues in Gottman and Silver (1999, pp. 187–216). Interestingly, they also found that those couples who maintained high expectations for the relationship, addressed conflict and refused to put up with negativity, ultimately had more satisfying relationships.

When a couple is stuck, Gottman (1999) emphasises the importance of dialogue. The issue is an indication that there are unrecognised dreams, aspirations, or values that are not recognised or valued by the other partner. Consider this case example:

> Tom wanted the new baby baptised in his Anglican faith; Amanda thought that this would hinder later choices by prematurely making a commitment to one expression of faith. The treating psychologist recommended that the couple talk more fully about their understandings of religion from their family-of-origin, and how they came to different adult understandings.

It is important to encourage the couple to reflect on what is the basis for their attitude rather than simply blame the partner for being different. The only way to make emotional progress is for the couple to accept the differences and 'declaw the issue' (Gottman & Silver, 1999, p. 234). Dreams may differ, but respect for the other can make all the difference.

After trying to understand each other's dreams, some helpful steps are for both to:

- define the minimal core areas that cannot be compromised
- identify areas of greater flexibility that are not so hot emotionally
- try to come up with a temporary compromise and plan.

One aspect of a longer-term relationship is that people become more accepting of the faults of the partner. A part of the pain of gridlock is feeling unaccepted and rejected; it helps to try to understand the other's view and accept it in spite of differences.

Gottman and Silver also recommend that couples find a shared meaning for their relationship 'that has to do with creating an inner life together — a culture rich with symbols and rituals, and an appreciation for ... roles and goals that link'. (1999, pp. 243–244). Shared meanings renew and enrich a relationship.

> ### To do
> Ask a couple what were the significant family rituals that were practised in their family-of-origin.

Thoughts about the termination of therapy

No relationship is ever free of problems; however, there does come a time when the couple can continue without the need of counselling. Usually 'enough' will be suggested by the psychologist or either of the couple. This is usually a recognition that progress has been made. What I would like to see is that the couple are managing conflict in a reasonably healthy way and that there is some sense of stability. What generally develops is an 'observer stance'. Either, and preferably both, will be better able to step back and observe what is happening in the relationship; not just react, but able to talk about what is happening.

I would also hope to see the couple better understand the emotional processes in their relationship: be aware of characteristic patterns, able to distinguish primary and secondary emotions, more competent at self-soothing, as well as at times helping the partner. Thus from an EFT-C perspective gains have been made and appear to be almost habitual in the relationship.

As I write this, I reflect on a final session I had with a couple in the previous hour. They were both more intentional about doing enjoyable things together, repairing when communication went astray, and observing how each characteristically handled life stresses in differing ways. I was delighted with the progress they had made over about six sessions. I ended with an agreement that I always propose: *I am happy to see you again at any time in the future that you feel stuck. Why don't we make an agreement that if either of you believes it is important to have another session, then the other agrees to come for one session? This is a two-way deal and no matter how you feel at the time, then you will both agree to come for that session. A deal?*

In the film *Parenthood* (1989), with comedian Steve Martin, there is a poignant scene near the end of the movie: the grandmother, whom everyone assumes to be somewhat senile, comes out with a wise metaphor of life. She contrasts life as either a merry-go-round or a rollercoaster. The patterns we have explored in this chapter are the merry-go-rounds of relationships, which ultimately go around and around. The rollercoaster is the difficult way of change.

When a relationship is under stress it is natural for each to project blame on to the other. When the expected responses are not forthcoming, the result is a feeling of powerlessness that leads to an inevitable 'stuckness'. But progress is possible only through self-focus and taking responsibility for constructive change. When an individual begins to define themselves there will be an initial rise in anxiety, which can lead to considerable turbulence. However, this can be a significant step towards a more satisfying relationship. The most effective way of self-defining is *in* the relationship.

Therapy with gay and lesbian couples

To this point, while most of the material on couple therapy is also applicable to gay and lesbian couples, it is also important to acknowledge and maintain the differences between heterosexual and gay and lesbian relationships. Many of these differences stem from gay and lesbian couples being part of a minority group, sometimes hidden and, still today, regrettably the target of societal judgment, ostracism, legal discrimination and, at times, verbal abuse and physical attack. This has implications for gay and lesbians as individuals in their development, social comfort and opportunities. There are also consequences for their relationships, including romantic, as well as with their families, friends and workmates. The following section focuses on gay and lesbian couples. It is mostly based on the papers of Jac Brown (2007), a clinical psychologist in Sydney, in which some of the key points are summarised. Brown argued that 'love is the same but intimacy is different'.

Gay and lesbian couples tend to form relationships when they are older. One contributing factor may be that gay and lesbian people have greater hurdles to overcome. Secrecy and stigma may lead to needing more time to develop a mature sense of self. Initially a gay person may need to form a very plausible peripheral self in order to hide sexual preference both from self and others. The effect of shame is profound for an invisible minority group, and members can go for a very long time without having this central part of themselves named, openly recognised, validated, and mirrored through peer experiences. Gay and lesbian people may go through years, if not their whole lives, dealing with external and, often, internalised self-hatred and homophobia. At the very least they have felt different, often have been bullied and probably traumatised. In this context it is much harder for young men or women to build a positive self-identity and self-esteem. In turn, this leads to later maturation, sexual social experimentation and ultimately, greater vulnerability in relationships.

Coming out is a major developmental stage for gay and lesbian people. Sometimes this occurs early in life and sometimes very late, and often within the context of a first liaison. The decision to come out is complex and difficult. For gay people, finding a partner is a bigger task, with fewer potential partners and perhaps less venues and occasions for meeting others — though after coming out this may become easier. Courage is a part of the journey to openly adopt a gay or lesbian lifestyle. Usually coming out is a step-by-step process, according to the safety of doing so in relevant work, occupational, social and family situations. The chance of development of a healthy sense of self can vastly improve if this process goes well and the person is welcomed with acceptance as a gay or a lesbian person. It is similar when gay and lesbian couples are accepted by the significant people in their lives.

When an individual or a couple are not out it is more difficult to be integrated into the general social life. Family often does not know and there are total or partial cut-offs. One parent might know, but not the other. Siblings might know, but not parents. When parents or families discover the true sexual preference of one of their members there is often a period of shock, denial, bargaining, self-blame, or gay blaming. If this mourning for the assumed heterosexuality can be processed, then family may become accepting of their gay and lesbian members as of other relationships. Sadly, this is not always the case. It is a terrible choice to have to choose between one's family and one's sexual preference. Without family as well as friends as supports, partners run the risk of relying predominantly on each other for emotional and other support. Inevitably this increases the importance and intensity of the relationship. Sometimes it is experienced as smothering. Diversity of connection, interests and activities are important for healthy, harmonious couple functioning. Friends in the gay and lesbian communities often become even more significant than in heterosexual circles as families-of-choice and relied upon for support and social contact.

Every new environment needs to be carefully assessed for the safety of being open. This vigilance may consume energy that could otherwise energise the relationship. It is not always safe to touch in public or be open about support in front of others. Words have to be carefully chosen. 'Partner' is the most commonly used gender-neutral term adopted.

One of the couple may be more open than the other. When this is the case, the more open may see it as an indication of lesser commitment to the relationship by the more closeted one. The degree of commitment can also be estimated from how the two partners handle 'we' conversations. Discussions about coming out in therapy can include examining the pros and cons of openness in each of the couple's relevant social settings, of separating the issue of love for the partner from the coming-out process and suggesting reading material about this process.

Issues of commitment are often a focus in therapy. For gay and lesbian people generally there is no social ceremony or legal or religious rite of passage that gives public recognition. Some couples devise their own occasions, bringing family and friends together. For other couples the significant event is establishing a home together or sharing financial arrangements. Many couples flocked to California in the United States for 'marriage' ceremonies when it was made legal there for same-sex people to marry. As soon as legal or religious possibilities open up for 'unions of two people' there is a big response. Lesbian and gay couples can see therapy together as a legitimising experience where they get the same treatment as other couples.

Gay and lesbian couples are more likely to break up in the first few years together, gay male couples being the most vulnerable, but in time their rate is the same as heterosexual relationships. The triggers for separation are the same as for heterosexual couples. Rates of domestic violence do not seem to vary between gay, lesbian or heterosexual couples. Couples with greater androgyny between the partners, a greater mix of stereotypically masculine or feminine traits, and gender role flexibility was correlated with couple harmony, as was the ability of influence each other's values and behaviours. This is the same with heterosexual couples.

Sexuality is important for all couples. Monogamy rates for gay and lesbian couples vary between research studies but most people have been in a long-term relationship at some point in their lives. For all couples, sexual frequency and satisfaction tends to decrease over time. Long-term gay male relationships, in particular, tend to be exclusive for the first five years and then often become open. Contrary to heterosexual relationships, this does not seem to threaten the primary bond and satisfaction between the partners. It is important that there are clearly articulated and negotiated rules followed by both partners. Ask in therapy if this is the case. Many couples have found that honesty and trust rather than monogamy are foundational for a good relationship.

The HIV/AIDS epidemic has had a big effect on the gay male community, which has had to deal with much loss and grief. There have been partners nursing the other until death. Safe-sex practices and sexual education have become highly emphasised. There are indications that the duration of gay relationships has increased because of health risks from casual sexual encounters. For lesbian couples the research shows that there is a high probability that at least one of the partners may have been sexually abused in her past.

Gay and lesbian couples may be parents, either because one or both partners have had previous heterosexual relationships and children, or have become parents by choice. In step-families the children may accept or resent their parent's change in sexual preference, as well as having many of the usual issues about their parents' split and re-partnering. Female partners may seek donors through a clinic or from friends. Male partners may adopt or may seek surrogate mothers. Male and female gays and lesbians may form one-couple-and-donor groupings in which a child might have three parents from birth. Some of these families have complex dynamics associated with these new family structures. For couples who may have wished to procreate but who have not been able to do so there may be issues of grief.

The role of the therapist is the same with gay and lesbian couples as with heterosexual couples. The sexual preference of the clinician may or may not be an issue. You may enquire if this is the case and discuss the matter. Some gay and lesbian couples may prefer a therapist who can identify with their issues, while others may prefer a straight therapist who is outside the gay and lesbian communities. Knowledge of, and comfort with, gay and lesbian issues and people are essential for the success of therapy. As usual, a psychologist's rapport and competence are essential ingredients.

In the next chapter, self-psychology is introduced and explored in relation to how it can be applied to couple therapy.

Chapter 10

Self-psychology and couples therapy: The building blocks for a focus on couple inter-affectivity

Couple and family therapy grew out of frustration with individual therapy in the search for more effective and briefer methods of intervention. Now the challenge is to integrate an understanding of the individual self with couple and family therapy. Clearly it is best to be constantly aware of the dialectic between the interactive and the intrapsychic (Burch & Jenkins, 1999). I found that the need to understand more about working with individuals came out of an awareness of the limitations of the couple, family and group frameworks. It is gratifying to notice, in recent years, a convergence between these different approaches.

Over the years there has been relatively little explicit attention paid to the meaning and use of specific emotions in family therapy. The most useful tips for me came from Kerrie James and Laurie MacKinnon during my Milan family therapy training in 1988. They were innovative in the tracking of emotional intensity in family interactions. This more or less guaranteed that the treating psychologist would be dealing with what was important for the family. However, while empathy has always been seen as crucial in the field of family therapy (Perry, 1993), I do not remember the subtleties of how to do this being discussed.

After reviewing the field, Gurman and Fraenckel (2002) noted their ironies about couple therapy:

> First, the *re-inclusion of the individual,* roughly equivalent to …
> the 'self in the system', may be the most far-reaching irony of all.
> As we have argued, couple therapy nearly died during the pure
> systems period of usurpation by family therapy. Johnson and
> Lebow (2000), in their recent decade review of marital therapy,
> identified the renewal of interest in affect (e.g., in EFT-C) as one of
> the major changes in recent years. We think that this important
> change reflects a much broader shift of perspective. It seems to
> express renewed interest in the psychology of the individual, not
> only in terms of affect, but also in terms of the cognitive-
> attributional elements of relationships, and even the capacity of
> individuals to influence relational systems by self-regulation.
> In this sense, then, we see it as strikingly ironic that while some
> very influential 'systems' therapies almost rang the death knell
> for couple therapy by largely disavowing the relevance of what
> occurs 'within' people in relationships, it is by the recent radical
> re-inclusion of the individual, by dealing with multiple levels of
> human experience, that couple therapy has become more
> genuinely systemic. (pp. 246–247)

In couple and family therapy we are forced to keep a firm grasp on the notion that there are multiple subjectivities. Working with people rather than a person, you get used to dealing with and holding intensity. The immediate reward for accurate empathy in this process potentially flows on to several people at once. Sometimes it is an easier, less demanding form of therapy, since the therapist is not immediately in the transference firing line. The intensity of the transference is generally between the partners rather than with the therapist (Crawley & Grant, 2008). The big advantage is in working directly with the couples' most important self-objects and lived experience.

Couple counselling is very 'alive' in every sense of the word. There is a lot at stake. Kohut (1971) emphasised the capacity to find rewarding adult relationships as a goal for healthy adult functioning. What is wrong will be quickly seen. Disjunctions, or breaks in empathic connection, happen directly in therapy with no need for a third-party account. There is considerable intensity. As Shaddock (2000) has noted, there is no transference as deeply felt in most adult lives as that experienced in an intimate relationship. It is not surprising that Schnarch (1997) described marriage a 'people growing machine', where each partner is confronted with themselves and the self of the partner, and is presented with the challenge of self-differentiation. The 'playing field' in some ways is surprisingly level. People normally choose spouses of similar levels of functioning as their own (Bowen, 1988). One person may look healthier than the other, but usually both operate with similar developmental gaps. The access to working with both partners at once is invaluable. It can save time and protect relationships.

This chapter begins with an introduction to self-psychology and then looks at models where it has been applied to couple therapy. Within these models I plan to expand on how the treating psychologist can focus on each partners' emotions. I will give an introduction to the importance of working in this way and look at some of the detailed approaches useful in couple therapy. I will include clinical illustrations of these from my work with couples.

Greenberg and Johnson (1988), Johnson (1996) and Greenberg and Goldman (2008) have written extensively in the area of therapy with couples focusing on emotion. Their work has echoes with a self-psychological approach but does not have a self-psychological underpinning. My hope is the present view will complement theirs and encourage readers to also become familiar with their work.

Self-psychology is based on the work of Heinz Kohut, an analyst sometimes called 'Mr Psychoanalysis', who practised in Chicago (Strozier, 2001). In the 1970s and 1980s, Kohut developed an analytic psychotherapy based on empathy in his work with patients with narcissistic personality disorders. In self-psychology, the primary concern is to understand the development of the self, the enhancement of healthy narcissism (or positive self-esteem), and naturally there is a focus on the individual's use of emotion (Kohut, 1971, 1977, 1984).

The self is the psychological and emotional core of each person's universe. It is the centre of the symbolising process and the centre of individual motivation. It is not a 'thing', but the stored record of emotional experiences over time. The self has a structure, an enduring organisation. Patterns of experience, layered and stored in the self, form the template against which further experiences are judged and interpreted. The self is the 'nuclear hierarchy of information processing' of an individual, the repository of this information and a centre of initiative and motivation for the individual (Kohut & Wolf, 1978).

The self is developed in an interpersonal context, usually between the infant and her mother or caretakers from its first minutes of life, and perhaps even in utero. The period from 0 to 2 years is particularly significant in the development of a sense of self (Stern, 1985). Briefly this consists of the infant using at first the mother as a self-object. For the infant a self-object is a source of soothing, admiration, belonging and information about their subjective self, emotions, and abilities as reflected in the parent's gaze, face, touch, voice and general behaviour. A parent, as a self-object, performs all those functions for the baby that the infant cannot perform. In this the infant's experience is of the self-object as one and the same as the self. Gradually the infant acquires the ability to independently perform these functions.

For example, in the acquisition of language the infant at first learns to recognise their mother's voice, then attending to affect, to recognise their own emotional patterns, and then to recognise the words that refer to each emotion, and finally, to use the words independently. A healthy developmental path allows a person to make secure connections with both intimate and non-intimate others, to develop abilities to soothe and quieten themselves, to develop and use natural skills and talents in the pursuit of goals and ideals, and to feel like they belong to a gender, to a family (and surrounding community). The self is the centre of initiative towards realistic and generally rewarding endeavours and when this process works well self-esteem is reasonably stable. The self is formed by genetic inheritance, parental, family, cultural and environmental factors.

Self-psychology and inter-subjectivity focus primarily on the subjective affective experience of human beings in dyadic relationships, be it a parent–child relationship, between members of a couple, within families, or in therapy between the patient and psychologist. The healthy self is one in which a person can deal with the vicissitudes of life with flexibility and resilience while maintaining a positive self-image and self-esteem despite challenges. There is a healthy process in which emotions are used as signals, can be articulated verbally and reflected upon and then assessed with an open mind. New and appropriate responses are found rather than relying on stereotyped and rigid or entrenched previous patterns, which are often defensive. The aim is development towards healthy, age-appropriate narcissism; in other words, positive self-esteem. It is a developmental model that assumes that each of us have reached the highest level of functioning possible given our self-object milieu. Everyone has gaps in development. Growth, although stymied or arrested, in the right relational environment can be reactivated and lead to actual new or compensatory structures, thereby enabling us to lead fuller and more emotionally satisfying lives.

Empathy is at the core of the therapeutic process. It involves putting oneself in another's shoes and trying to understand their experience from inside, as well as providing them with the response most useful to their development. The two main foci of empathy in therapy are self-object needs and emotions. Stolorow, Brandshaft, and Atwood (1995) have noted that therapy is 'the analyst's attunement to the patient's emotional states and developmental needs' (p.101). The process of cure relies on understanding, describing a patient's experience, connecting different aspects, explaining it and, lastly, interpreting in the process of helping to form the structures of a functional self.

Self-object needs are interpersonal needs, ranging from the immature forms in infancy to the mature of later life. These are ubiquitous, including between parent and child, within families, indeed between any two people. They are two self-systems eliciting responses from one another. Both sides of the interaction have self-object needs being met. Socarides and Stolorow (1984) noted 'self-object functions pertain fundamentally to the integration of affect and that the need for self-objects pertains most centrally for phase appropriate responsiveness to affect states in all stages of the life cycle'. Gordon (1987) claimed that self-objects allow for the integration affect through the naming of the affect, the validation of the affect, the assimilation of the impact of the affect, and the modulation of it. The opposite of this means that caregivers ignore, oppose affects, react negatively to affects, and even punish their display.

McWilliams (1999) described what can go wrong in families and how therapists can offer alternative, positive, structure-building experiences if caregivers:

- neglect feelings — it is the job of the therapist to welcome and show interest in feelings
- name feelings in a tone of negative judgment — the therapist then names those feelings nonjudgmentally
- punish children for feeling — the therapist encourages safe emotional expression
- make inaccurate distortions of feelings — it is important for the therapist to name feelings accurately (this is actually the hardest of the four).

There is a universal need for education about emotion and witnesses, namers and validators of feelings. Therapy should provide a stable and warm relationship, firm boundaries, handling of protest, reliability, and emotional responsiveness that assist with affect regulation — aspects of a secure attachment bond (Crawley, 1998; Crawley & Grant, 2002).

It is highly likely that clinicians of all theoretical perspectives provide self-object functions to their patients. However, understanding self-object functions and transferences enable us to be more purposeful and perhaps more comfortable in providing what is needed. For example, being highly idealised can be uncomfortable, particularly to psychologists early in their careers, or if they have been formed by approaches that seek to avoid the expert role. Learning to predict and accept this patient need is likely to help both sides of the process. The three self-object transferences and the developmental tasks they are meant to address are as follows (Kohut, 1971, 1977, 1984):

1. *Idealising* is typified by the child looking up at the parent as a source of calmness, consistency, security, values, and wisdom. The outcome of this self-object function is the structuralisation of the child's ability to self-soothe, self-regulate, develop ideals, trust, admiration for others and respect for their knowledge. It is the antidote for the affects of distress, anxiety, fear, vulnerability and confusion.

2. *Mirroring* is crucial for children to learn about themselves, their qualities, talents and affect states, including pride, expansiveness, efficacy and pleasurable excitement. Mirroring is crucial for the development of healthy self-esteem, ambitions and talents, competence and mastery. According to Stern (1985) it includes three components: (a) reflecting back, or attention to and imitation of behaviour, (b) alignment of emotional states or affect attunement, and (c) verbal reinforcement. Thus, the person mirroring goes beyond participating in the child's affective experience to offering the child something that was not previously there — a representation of their experience through another's response to and with it.

3. *Twinship* or *alter ego* self-object function is part of our human need to feel we belong to the human race, to a gender, to an age group, to a family, to a region and to a culture. We have a need to resemble a sufficient number of other human beings. Parents who are able to twin their children accept their child's

assertive affection and competition, and do not see this as dangerous aggression and sexuality. While parents originally perform the other functions, the twinship or belonging aspects of family is shared by siblings within a family (Shaddock, 2000).

Brighton-Cleghorn (1987) summarised these three sets of relational needs in her words as 'What is hidden in some developmentally arrested individuals and families are longings for more perfect experiences of belonging, of merging with a greater one; or longing for more perfect reflective experiences of themselves as unique, distinct, and special: or a sense of missing twinship/ alter-ego experiences of shared humanness and likenesses' (pp. 190–191). In couple therapy the missing self-object experiences initially may be provided to each individual by the treating psychologist, and as therapy proceeds the partners are able to take over this these roles with each other.

The case of Rose and Julian illustrates the movement from individual therapy to couple therapy. At first, I served as an idealising self-object to Rose and then coached her to become a self-object to Julian, and then she brought him to join us in therapy. Ringstrom (1994) described a six-step model of conjoint therapy using a self-psychological framework. In the therapeutic relationship hope and perspective are renewed by:

1. attuning to both patients
2. describing a view that each perspective and subjectivity is valid within a relationship and is not mutually exclusive
3. showing that each partner's pain, fear, shame and disappointment originate from developmental and family of origin patterns and perspectives, in existence long before the partners met each other, but currently interacting with each other's views and experience of relationships
4. illustrating how each partner keeps a sense of themselves in the present as a result of these earlier influences by gravitating towards behaviour and coping mechanisms that help to maintain it

5. enhancing each partner's capacity to each look at their own issues in the face of a partner with issues of their own, without diminishing their sense of self or that of their partner (e.g., avoiding either blaming themselves or accommodating to their partner)

6. facilitating each partner's emotional availability and self-object function to their partner and allowing space for their respective self-esteem and growth. This is possible with couples who have a reasonably strong and coherent sense of self. Patients with more fragile structures probably need individual therapy before helping them attune to a partner.

Tom Young (unpublished paper, 2001), refined Ringstom's work (1994), and listed 10 steps he uses working with couples:

1. identifying and providing the self-object needs of both members of a couple

2. understanding each person's emotions and their need for self-regulation

3. moving the couple from mutual shaming and blaming into a reframed, no-fault couple narrative

4. understanding and naming the reciprocal injuring and defensive dynamics between partners

5. linking these painful sequences to family-of-origin patterns and connecting to distant past causality for present hurt

6. helping with the mourning of loss of opportunity as a result of parental misattunement

7. encouraging, even coaching couples, to explore alternative more satisfying interactions

8. emphasising that each partner be empathic with the other and transforming this into supportive, coherent patterns of relating

9. helping both partners to develop skills and experience of intimate connection

10. enabling partners to prove to themselves that intimacy does not entail a loss of self.

In the treatment of Rose and Julian, individual therapy led into interweaving individual and couple therapy. Rose was describing situations in which her husband would react as if she had said to him he was not good enough, look hurt and withdraw from her for days.

Despite her considerable knowledge about her husband's background and her own psychological sophistication she had not been able to make sense of it. I asked her about her husband's upbringing and whether he had had a strict or critical parent. He seemed to be having a reaction out of proportion to what Rose asked of him. She recalled that his father had been a very critical man. After a long illness, his mother had died when Julian was young and somehow Julian felt to blame. After this realisation she discussed it with her husband. The pattern finally allowed them to understand Julian's responses to Rose. He was able to differentiate her suggestions or requests from his previous emotional arousal. With the relief that this insight brought him, his scepticism about treatment lessened. He decided to come to individual therapy with me.

This move towards helping Rose look beyond her own needs and focus on understanding that Julian's behaviour stemmed from events predating their relationship. It helped Rose to become available to him as an accepting 'idealising' self-object, a new role in their marital system.

Their discussions took a more productive path in which she no longer felt ignored or neglected and he could see that she was not criticising him but asking him for reasonable cooperation. The genetic explanation for his pattern changed the negative view of her input and diminished his own shame and helplessness.

Later in the treatment of this couple, both individual and joint therapy were used simultaneously with the same therapist for each modality. Interweaving individual and couple therapy is professionally controversial in some circles. I will acknowledge this debate but focus here on the merits of combining the two. Burch and Jenkins (1999) asserted that 'adjunctive therapies coexist well' and I am inclined to agree with them. This also seems to be the practical experience of many clinicians in the field (Lebow, 1997).

Rose and Julian started what I will call adjunct, interwoven therapies with me. Rose addressed past family trauma and grief. This recently had manifested itself in paralysing grief after the loss of her cherished pets. Julian dealt with issues of post-traumatic stress, issues from his first marriage and family as well with an unfair work dismissal.

As a therapist I served as an idealising self-object for each of them. Together they focused on their own interaction doing quite a lot of this work at home, but bringing more difficult issues to joint sessions. One of these concerned Julian's rapprochement to his oldest daughter overseas. Notions of the importance and power of family loyalty (Boszormenyi-Nagy & Ulrich, 1981) have been the keys for Julian to decentre from his own painful perspective, understand that his daughter has elected to not see him, her estranged father, as his visit coincided with her mother's 60th birthday celebrations.

I pointed out that his daughter would have felt emotionally torn by loyalty ties. However, she would understandably side with her mother who had brought her up, and who would have been devastated if she had done otherwise. Julian was able, with Rose's support, to accept his daughter's choice without communicating to her his hurt and rancour. Instead, also shifting into a self-object role or a more differentiated mode, Julian wrote to his daughter and told her that he understood her dilemma. Naturally her mother's celebration came first. He would still be spending a few days in her hometown and hoped that maybe she might find a moment to see him despite her other commitments. Either way, he told her, he was glad they were in contact.

He was happy to answer her questions about his side of the divorce from her mother.

Rose and Julian were able to go on their trip without apprehension. They felt proud and confident in the manner of tackling what had loomed as a threatening issue. The daughter responded warmly to Julian's letter and repeated that her current decision was only temporary and that she hoped to see him in the future.

In the next section I will cover some of the refinement in understanding emotions in general followed by how these can be useful in detailed work with couples inter-affectivity. The main areas of focus are:

- which emotions are in evidence between partners and which are missing?
- which emotions are 'intimacy' emotions for the couple and for their respective partners families of origin?
- whether the emotions displayed achieve the desired goals for each partner. Are core-self or peripheral-self emotions on display? Are the crucial emotions the ones that are showing?

Emotions form our primary, nonverbal signal system from birth. They are the earliest mammal and human mode of communication. Our goal as the human species is to survive as individuals and with each other as families and communities over time. Emotions form the system by which as organisms we appraise our environment and determine if it is useful, harmful or neutral (Siegel, 1999). They motivate us to act in accordance with the environment to insure our survival and wellbeing. Emotions help us connect, organise, and operate as a social species (Haidt, 2001; Pinker, 2002). In the last 15 years there has been an explosion of interest, writing and research about emotions, their neurophysiology and function, and their interaction with and relationship to cognitive processes (Damasio, 2000; LeDoux, 1996; Lee, 2000; Linehan, 1993; Panksepp, 1998; Pinker, 2002; Schore, 1994; Siegel, 1999; Tomkins, 1962, 1963, 1991, 1992).

'I feel therefore I am' is the defining statement for our human experience, not the Cartesian 'I think therefore I am' (Panksepp, 1998). The right side of the brain, the seat of emotional functioning, develops before the left rational side. Under stress the signals from the limbic system up to the cortex are dominant over the flow in the opposite direction. Emotions are primary. As Haidt (2001) has said: 'Affective evaluation occurs so quickly, automatically, and pervasively that it is generally thought to be an integral part of perception. The affective primacy has primacy in every sense: It came first in phylogeny, it emerges first in ontogeny, it is triggered more quickly in real-time judgments, and it is more powerful and irrevocable when the two systems yield conflicting judgments' (p. 819).

Siegel (1999) noted: 'Though emotion can be defined as a subjective experience involving neurobiological, experiential, and behavioural components, it is in fact the essence of the mind. Emotional communication is also the fundamental manner in which one mind connects to another' (p. 275). Emotion, and its regulation, has always been the concern of therapy as patients present various forms of affect dis-regulation, including emotions (too much or too little), such as depression, grief, anxiety, post-traumatic stress disorder (PTSD), anger, rage, terror and shame.

Emotional health and self-esteem are distinguished by our ability to be self-reflective and empathic, to be humorous (but not sarcastic or cynical), to be creative, wise, and to be accepting of death. The whole self is harmonious, alive, flexible in responsiveness, well connected to others, and has a sense of unfolding in an orderly, understandable way over time (Kohut, 1984). For any of us to have these capacities we need to have had sufficient self-object function richness in infancy (Kohut & Wolf, 1978).

All emotions with moderation are useful, and are necessary at optimal levels of stimulation. Magai (1999), with input from Tomkins (1962, 1963, 1991, 1992) and Bowlby (1969, 1973, 1980), described secure attachment and exploration as being exemplified by (a) differentiated affective experience, (b) maximising positive affect, (c) minimising negative affect, (d) minimising affect inhibition, and (e) achievement of a feeling of efficacy. These result for us is ideo-affective organisations or scripts, which are rules and strategies that allow us to order, interpret, evaluate, predict and control affectively laden scenes or events.

Which emotions are in evidence between partners and which are not?

There can be more sophistication in empathising with patients than what we were taught in basic counselling courses — tentatively repeating back their stated feelings. There is more than the tracking of emotions, the circumstances of their manifestation as proposed by the brief therapy solution focused approach to emotion (Miller & de Shazer, 1998). The greater the number of primary emotions that are present, displayed and articulated the less problematic is the individual's or the couple's emotional life. A family in which only three or four of the primary emotions can be comfortably acknowledged is emotionally impoverished. Emotions are part of our ability to function and to navigate safely through life, indeed to survive. To know how to identify, interpret, use and channel our emotions, and as many as possible of them, is essential to our wellbeing. There are nine key emotions: the three primary or reptilian ones: interest, distress, startle/surprise; three old mammalian ones: anger, fear and joy; three new mammalian ones: shame, contempt/disgust, and dismell (Lee, 2000; Tomkins, 1962, 1963, 1991, 1992).

- *Interest/excitement* is the earliest to appear. It is attached to perceptual and conceptual-cognitive affective system. This needs a mirroring response. It is part of our essential 'seeking system' (see Panksepp, discussed later). The parental or therapist's interest leads to energising. Along with joy, guilt, and shame it is associated with secure attachment (Magai, 1999). In couples with one depressed partner, the energy drains from the system as there is no interested mirroring response by the depressed partner to the other and the depressed partner fails to be re-energised by the well partner.

- *Startle/surprise* is even pre-reptilian. It overrides attention to anything else. New, sudden and intense stimuli elicit this response. With repetition the organism habituates to them. This is the origin of self-regulation. People without the ability to habituate may be traumatised or severely impaired. For example, people with schizophrenia often feel like they are on permanent alert. In therapy it is useful to interpret the connection between past and present to show that the person is reacting in the present as if to past alarming situations. This difficulty can also be the result of an innate, extra sensitivity to certain stimuli, sounds, sight, touch, which needs modulation first by a caregiver then, increasingly by the child on his or her own. Over or under reaction of one partner to another can lead to over or under stimulation between them. A woman recently told me she left a relationship because her partner suffered from PTSD and was so reliant on her presence for soothing that she could not do anything independently from him. It the end this became suffocating.

- *Distress* is the signal that invites rescue, comfort, attachment and protection. It can be allowed to run its course. In therapy distress needs to be accepted and shared. It is an emotion important in the development of twinship and bonding within a family. There are likely to be problems in families where the display rules don't allow for its expression. There are also gender differences, making it harder for boys and men to admit distress and to elicit adequate comforting. For some men it is unmasculine to ever rely on a partner for comfort, hence they never show distress. This eventually affects closeness in the couple relationship.

- *Joy/excitement* is an experience of the whole person. It enhances bonding and needs to be mirrored and joined in celebration. Along with guilt and shame, the expression of joy in families is associated with secure attachment (Magai, 1999). It is a total self-experience in which pleasure pertains to parts of the self. In therapy, making time to share it is experienced as empathic. Therapy benefits from a balanced focus on the positive as well as the negative emotions. It is sad when on occasion I have found patients who are so narcissistically preoccupied that they react to a partner's joy at achievement with denigration, withdrawal or competitiveness.

- *Fear/terror* requires a calm/idealising response from a caregiver or therapist. It is the basis for keeping the organism safe, intact and alive. It prepares the body to survive by freezing, fleeing or fighting. Self-soothing is greatly helped by describing it to another person. Again a patient who, for example, is overwhelmed by unarticulated fear due to PTSD after a rape, might withdraw and communicate rejection to their spouse, instead of eliciting reassurance.

- *Anxiety* is related to fear/terror, but it is aroused in relation to needs not being met (hunger, sleep, safety). It is a precursor of other feelings such sexual arousal and interest. It circles around experiences of competence, acceptability, abandonment or engulfment. Anxiety is also a breakdown product of the fragmented self, a self experiencing serious threat. It is manifest in anticipation of events threatening to the self. Wolf (1980) wrote 'Solitude, psychological solitude, is the mother of anxiety'. Anxiety from a Bowen perspective (Kerr, 1981) is a sign of the fusion of the emotional and the intellectual systems. His view of anxiety fits well within a self-psychological perspective in that it signals a breakdown in the person's ability to be in charge of their functioning. In families it appears when there is fear by members of too much or too little contact or connection. In working with poorly differentiated or highly anxious systems it is important for the therapist to not become a stabilising third person in a triangle but to be available to understand and reflect on the emotions of all members, including the couple. Anxiety is present in couples where there is fear of suffocation on one end and of abandonment or rejection on the other. This is the core of the pursuer–distancer dynamic central to many writers in the field (Hendrix, 1988; King, 1998).

- *Anger/rage* is aimed at getting others to go away or to punish them. Anger is an affect that accumulates over time. A small trigger can release rage so it appears to be a major injury. Anger that is not eruptive and violent is attenuated by an empathic response. At a low range, anger is a good motivator. A constructive approach to anger is to understand what triggers it and to channel the energy into constructive self-enhancing assertive action (Lee, 2000, p. 254). Livingston (1998) agrees with Kohut (1984) that: 'Legitimise the underlying vulnerability of each person's self, expressed and explored to facilitate a curative process' (Livingston, 1998, p. 312). Livingston (1998) warned that with couples one needs to create safety before this is possible. He also pointed out the need to do this with the reactions of the other parties in mind — their narcissistic vulnerability, susceptibility to fragmentation and their fear of loss of the relationship if anger or even assertiveness is expressed. Anger can be a cover for more painful feelings, a distraction used by batterers, for example, to avoid or mitigate shame, humiliation, guilt, fear of abandonment (McWilliams, 1999, p. 113). Therapists need to be able to differentiate between hot, immediate rage as opposed to the cold, calculating rage of a psychopath. Anger is a useful emotion if verbally expressed in a responsible way. Often with couples, we see instances of the verbally or physically aggressive expression of anger. Indeed, the destructive expression of anger is a problem in most of the couples presenting for therapy. Narcissistic rage is a breakdown product, a secondary reactive result for a fragmentation-prone self. It manifests after an event that threatened the self. It follows narcissistic injury or overstimulation as a result of insults to grandiosity or of traumatic disappointments by an idealised self-object. In therapy it is useful to explore the meanings of the disjunction, to accept, understand, and interpret the conflict as an expectable reaction to actual or fantasised slights. It is also very useful to focus on what it feels like for the person to be angry. Magai (1999) claimed that anger, along with sadness, is associated with fear/avoidant attachment. The goal is to transform narcissistic rage and hurt into assertive and purposeful action (Lee, 1998). In working with couples there is a need to validate the needs of the rage-filled party at the same time as the emotional effect of being the target of the rage for the person on the receiving end (Livingston, 1998).

• *Shame/humiliation* results from not living up to ideals and from a lack of mirroring. Basch (1992, p. 67) said: 'Shame is the inner response often experienced when the reaction we anticipate and/or hope for is not forthcoming'. Siegel (1999) differentiated shame from humiliation where the parent fails to repair a disconnection or remains angry in a sustained way. Shame is the result when excessive grandiosity produces deflation and defensive contractedness. People literally hide or split off the shameful emotions, and hence are out of touch with them. Siegel (1999) and Schore (1994) argued that shame is a cover for other painful affects. Lee (2000) maintained that shame, the reverse of mirroring, results from a total lack of interest and is about failing to live up to ideals. In therapy the goal is not to uncover the shame, but to identify unworkable ideals and set more realistic goals. It is not often necessary to name shame for the client. When explained, others can describe shame as an internal state, not as condemnation. These moves are likely to be experienced as empathic. Interestingly, in balance with interest and joy, shame is found to be associated with secure attachment (Magai, 1999). Scheff (1994) has suggested that shame is the master socialising affect because of its powerful interpersonal pull. Earlier, Tomkins (1963) noted that within the parent–child relationship, shame is elicited in the child by the experience of defeat. Contemptuous communications by parents, including derogatory, derisory, belittling comments or tone of voice, and physical displays of disgust and contempt also elicit shame. The use of contempt to induce shame is one of the most common and powerful means of achieving control over social behaviour. It also has the most negative side-effects because it is so punitive, rejecting and distancing. In working with families the reciprocity of the disgust/shame cycle needs to be monitored and often interrupted. Gottman (1999) listed the presence of contempt as one of the predictors of separation for couples but maybe it should be the presence of the interactive contempt/shame dynamic where there is contempt for one partner and complementary shame in the other.

• *Disgust* is the emotion that evolved from our primitive need to keep safe from contaminated substances, and is thought to be the origin of moral judgement, ideas of purity and good health (Haidt, 2001). Disgust is about pushing unacceptable objects away. It helps us discriminate among people with whom we do and do not want to be associated. It is about avoiding poisonous situations, taking the high moral ground, being sarcastic and cynical, name-calling, eye-rolling, mocking, and interrupting others. It is part of the channel that contains anger. An excess of it is present in people with severe emotional disorders. The antidote to disgust, contempt and dismell (Lee, 2000) of others is to find traits in others to respect — to think of their positive qualities, to find fondness if not admiration for them. Disgust of one partner for the other's physical appearance or sexuality can play a major part in couple difficulties.

• *Contempt* is a milder form of disgust. McWilliams (1994) noted that for narcissistically vulnerable patients contempt is part of their defence against shame and against admitting they need mirroring. It is an attempt to build up their self-esteem by comparing themselves favourably with others. For these people the therapeutic strategy is to quietly note the affect and to take a realistic attitude towards their own shortcomings, to remain empathic, and patiently serve as a self-object. Admitting mistakes and repairing disjunctions in a matter-of-fact way can be very beneficial to them. The presence of contempt is part of a poor prognosis for couples (Gottman, 1999).

- *Dismell* (Lee, 2000) is about keeping away from others at the slightest whiff of malodour. Although there is not much in the professional literature about it, the 1986 novel *Perfume* by Patrick Suskind is a fascinating exploration of this topic. For the hero, being born with no body odour or personal smell presents him with extreme difficulty. He finds that people do not notice him and this make it very hard for him to relate in any way to them. It is quite possible that the dynamics of dismell are similar to those of disgust, and that both disgust and dismell forms dismell/shame, a similar complementarity to disgust or contempt/shame.

There are dozens of descriptions of emotional states in all their subtleties, gradations and combinations. Some combinations of emotions are grouped into affect complexes. Here are some that patients often present with in therapy:

- *Depression* consists of a mixture of distress, shame, anger turned in on the self, disgust and dismell. Clinically, it is useful to explore the relevant component affects and to show interest and respect in seeking to understand them. Magai (1999) said that depression is associated with dismissive attachment. McWilliams (1999) argued that depression needs to be converted into mourning. Psychotherapy is the process of helping people to come to terms with life's realities. We can recognise when difficulties result from external factors rather than from personal failings, while accepting that they are the main agents of change in our lives. A patient may eventually need to allow the therapist to leave the idealised position and to experience more equality with them as a part of building self-esteem. This echoes with Young's (2001) sixth step when working with couples (mentioned earlier). This was particularly evident with one of my couples in treatment. The wife discovered that most of her frustrations with her husband were probably due to undiagnosed Asperger's syndrome. She had to come to terms with his limitation in being unable to serve as a mirroring self-object for her as he was very poor at reading emotions. This realisation enabled her to mourn this fact instead of remaining depressed, angry, frustrated and hurt by his lack of responsiveness to her needs throughout their marriage. It is fortunate that the Australian Psychological Society and Medicare in Australia recognise that couple therapy is recommended for such cases.

- *Grief* is the mix of sadness and distress. It is different from depression in which, unlike the loss of a significant other, there is the perceived diminishment of self and an emptiness of the self. With grief there is an emptiness of the world, not of the person (McWilliams, 1999). Grief is the process by which we come to terms with the finiteness of life and with our limitations as human beings. It helps us come to terms with inevitable disappointments. People in grief find repeatedly sharing it helpful. One patient came from a family where her mother could never share grief, even the grief over the death of her husband, the patient's father, which indicated a lack of idealising self-object function. On asking her mother why this was so she discovered that her maternal grandmother was widowed very young in a culture where showing any tender emotions — hurt, grief, fear and distress — was considered a sign of weakness. A highlight of this woman's own marriage was her husband's kind acceptance and caring attention to her when her mother died, which provided an appropriate self-object function. She was also struck by the fact that her own sister had not been so lucky in her marriage. Her brother-in-law had insisted that the sister start disposing of her mother's belongings the day after the funeral. My client claimed that it had been very hard for her not to bristle and interfere to defend her sister's right to grieve at her own pace.

- *Envy* is a negative emotion full of hate, resentfulness and desire to possess or ruin positive qualities seen in another (Wahba, 1991). It includes shame of oneself for being inadequate when faced with the living example of someone who has attributes, achievements or experiences one cannot have.

In envy, distress is disavowed as are the disgust and dismell for the envied person. Envy involves the experience of a negative twinship. In includes anger and the desire to destroy and/or humiliate the other (Bayley & Lee, 2002). Treatment to address envy will focus on finding positive twinship experiences for the patient, including with the therapist. Interpreting envy to the envious individual is not advisable. Instead the patient's behaviour needs to be understood within their context and history. The experience of joy for another is hard for the person to accept, particularly if they have been a reverse self-object or, in family therapy terms, a parentified child, deprived of their own experiences of joy, perhaps also the subject of envious parental attacks. Facilitating the validation of these needs and the mourning of missed self-object experiences is the goal of therapy. In modern marriages, envy is often present in situations in which one partner envies the other's situation. Career women envy their partners' ability to have it all — career and family — where they, as mothers, have to choose between these two life paths as it is very difficult to be fully engaged in both to the degree that they would like. Men at times envy women this choice. For either, this dynamic can be more insidious in the relationship if there has been a pattern of envy from their own parents. In this case envy may be destructive of each other's efforts. A husband might sabotage a frustrated career wife's efforts to return to work or she might claim for herself the children's affections and alliances and be accusatory of his inadequate parenting. Untangling in therapy such trails of emotions and needs can help each partner articulate more clearly their own dilemmas, with the aim of coming to a more cooperative and validating relationship providing a mirroring self-object function.

- *Guilt* results from the breaking of an individual's moral code. Lewis (1992) argued that guilt is about part of the person, in contrast with shame, which involves the whole person. McWilliams (1999) distinguished between guilt and shame-based perfectionism. In the first case the person is obsessive and needs to be perfect, in control for fear of their aggressive-ness and anger making a mess of things. In the second, or shame-based perfectionism, the person is afraid of exposure, of being found incompetent or fraudulent. Guilt can be strongest in families with excessively strict codes of conduct, and also in families with severely insufficient parenting in which children have been left to develop their own guidelines for behaviour. Such children tend to have standards that are amazingly harsh. In therapy, an idealising transference allows for the development of more reasonable moral guidelines. This is a delicate process when the patient is very attached to, or takes great pride in, their superior standards. McWilliams (1999) has observed that the dynamics of guilt vary consider-ably across personality configurations. Her work described the sophistication that treatment addressing guilt can entail. In dual career marriages with children, both parents often carry guilt about the perceived insufficient input to their chil-dren. Sometimes this manifests in not spending any time in couple activities and renewal. There may be a material overindulgence of the spouse or children in an effort to com-pensate for a lack of time together. Often helping such couples realise that others in their situation face the same dilemmas and struggles diminishes the stress of their guilt (by provid-ing a twinship self-object function). One might as well 'give them permission' (therapist as idealising self-object function) to give up on being 'super-mums and -dads' and to employ cleaners, gardeners, babysitters in order for there to be more coupling or family time.

Which emotions are 'intimacy' emotions for the couple and their respective partner's families of origin?

Gordon (1987, p. 171) stated:

> commonly the emotions most frequently and intensely shared are those of interest, enjoyment and surprise ... However, in some mother/infant dyads ... fear, anger, distress, shame, contempt or disgust may take central roles ... Intensify the interactions that

> exist around a particular affect and my definition of 'intimacy'
> comes to the fore, the mother tongue, the intense experience,
> perhaps the core experience linking mother and child and
> providing an intense bond of feeling. It is to this bond that the
> patient returns over and over again in an attempt to feel 'at home'.
> (p. 5)

Gordon (1987) gives an example of a patient who always came to sessions in a dishevelled condition. Over the course of time they discovered that the only time his mother would cease her relentless criticism of him was when he was unwell, unkempt and distraught. She would then hold her child close and comfort him. The client was repeating a version of this pattern with his therapist.

Gordon's (1987) description of such repetition of intense affects and the interactions surrounding them seems to tie in with MacKinnon and James's (1987) notion of tracking family patterns of behaviour centring on peaks of emotional intensity.

Couple therapy provides us with real opportunities for unravelling and rescripting such nodes of affect. Required self-object experiences can be structured simultaneously for one, if not all, of the family members present. In regard to the sequence of affective displays, Stern (1985) wrote that joyful display can be followed by parental nonverbals that shape subsequent displays by the child. For example, a parent who looks depressed will have one affect, while one who seems disgusted will have quite another. In therapy, tracking and relating to sequences can deepen a patient's sense of being understood. Identifying a repeating pattern of emotions is likely to help family members feel understood. With couples, for example, I often describe the reciprocal and escalating effect of the partners' defensive behaviour and the resulting feelings about each other. Once this kind of pattern is described they can begin to examine it as a phenomenon over which they might have some control.

I recall working with a couple in which there was considerable conflict over the lack of time spent together talking and sharing the day's events. They had met as participants in the same sport, but played on different teams in gender-specific competitions. She did not want as much time-sharing as he did and could not understand. In exploring their respective families of origin we discovered that each of them had had the most intense relationship in the family with a sibling. She had been the second born of identical twins in a large family in which her elder twin was very intrusive and competitive with her. She resented her twin needing to copy and always exceed her in every interest she took on. She would always want to know what my patient was doing and later as an adult became less and less inclined to tell her sister much at all about her life. Her husband, on the other hand, had come from a separated family, in which he and his sister had been the two most constant companions in each other's lives throughout a childhood of being shuttled between two functional but separate parental homes. Recently, contact with this sister had become severely limited as she had married a man who required exclusive attention, and who felt threatened by their closeness as siblings. He had sought this closeness with his wife, understandably enough, but with perhaps greater than expected disappointment when it did not occur. She in turn, perhaps more strongly as a result of her twin's intrusiveness, became more and more adamant that she needed space and did not see the need for this type of regular interaction. This new perspective for the couple freed up each of them within themselves, and with each other, to look at ways of both stating their needs and acknowledging those of their partners. They moved from behaviourally enacting their emotional needs to being able to recognise, label and communicate them verbally. This is an example of a couple with a classic pursuer–distancer pattern (see step 3 in Ringstrom, 1994, and step 5 for Young, 2001), a step that in my experience is more often than not the turning point in widening a couple's understanding of their relationship, and releasing them from the unconscious pull of the intensity patterns of their families of origin.

Do the emotions displayed achieve the desired goals for each partner? Are core-self or peripheral-self emotions on display? Are the crucial emotions the ones that are showing?

Haidt (2001) said that the empathy aroused by perception of someone else's suffering evokes an altruistic motivation directed toward the ultimate goal of reducing suffering. If we cannot feel, or estimate what others feel, we are not moved to connect with them or to care for them. Psychopaths know social rules, but they cannot anticipate what emotions others might feel and cannot connect emotionally with others. What drives such socially deviant people are their own needs, and so they cannot give to another person but have to deceive and manipulate others into satisfying their limited emotional cravings. Haidt (2001) described emotions as helping us to weave our moral and social fabric. It is easy to extrapolate the importance of this concept for couple interaction. Emotions are categorised into:

- other shaping or condemning/avoiding: contempt, anger, disgust, and [I add] dismell
- other shaping or praising: gratitude, moral awe, and admiration, being moved and [I add] interest, joy
- other suffering and[I add] other-helping: compassion, sympathy, empathy
- self-conscious or self-monitoring emotions: guilt, shame and embarrassment.

Families can be dysfunctional if one of these modes is minimal or missing. We have all seen patients whose parents have been too critical and punishing and those who have not had enough positive validation, direction or limit setting.

Panksepp (1998), in his neurologically based taxonomy of emotional processes, listed six functions that our emotions serve. He divided them into these systems:

1. *Seeking system*, which is constituted by the search for food, water, warmth, evacuation, and bodily comfort; and by the

need for social contact, goal-directed behaviour, showing interest and curiosity in the environment.

2. *Rage system* that energises the body to angrily defend its territory and resources and is triggered by frustration or being thwarted. This emotion is used in boundary setting, self-protection and at lower levels of intensity in self-assertion.

3. *Fear system* that organises the body into flight, fight or freeze modes, and keeps it safe from pain and or destruction.

4. *Panic system* that generates bonding and is the opposite to, and the remedy for states of loneliness, separation, distress and grief. It brings people nearer as suppliers of care and comfort.

5. *Lust, care and play system*, which is the system for sexual and parental feelings. It includes the urge to express oneself vigorously, socially, including through rough and tumble play.

6. *Dominance system* that orders interactions and helps some individuals assert control over others.

In couples and families each of these systems can be observed in operation and each is necessary. There can be problems when panic doesn't bring comforting from partners as with parents when anger does not generate respect for boundaries, when joy, play and creativity are not part of family interaction, or when children consistently have more dominance in what the family does than parents do.

There are different approaches to understanding distortions in the communication of feelings, intentions and needs. McWilliams (1999) asked how the patient uses affects defensively. Which are the cover feelings for more uncomfortable ones? For example, anger can cover fear, distress or shame. Shame can hide distress, anger, pleasure, joy, excitement, envy or guilt. Greenberg and Johnson (1988) and Linehan (1993) have thought about primary versus secondary emotions in their work with couples. The idea is to focus directly on the most intense emotion and hence move from the covering emotion to the unattended underlying one. It is very useful to move from secondary anger (a distancing or boundary forming emotion) to hurt or fear (those primary emotions that are much more likely to engender closeness, support and connection).

Defences can be strategies used to regulate uncomfortable emotions. There is a wealth of psychoanalytic literature about defences. McWilliams (1994) grouped defences into primary ones (denial, primitive withdrawal; omnipotent control, primitive idealisation or devaluation; projection, introjection and projective identification, splitting and dissociation), and secondary ones (regression, isolation, intellectualisation, rationalisation, moralisation, compartmentalisation, undoing, turning against the self, displacement, reversal, identification, acting out, sexualisation and sublimation). Her work contains lucid descriptions of how they operate in emotional self-regulation.

In the last case example of a pursuer–distancer couple, he defended from his fear of abandonment by pursuing his wife, wanting regular times for intimate talking, and she defended her fear of invasion or engulfment by avoiding these occasions.

Greenberg and Johnson (1988) focused on underlying feelings. Anger is often, for men in particular, a cover for vulnerability and fear — a secondary emotion. Generally, the expression of aggressive anger will lead to more distance in the relationship. When vulnerability, a primary emotion, can be expressed, closeness is much more likely to be a partner response. In the case I described, each of the partners began to understand each other's underlying feelings and became closer as a result.

Feelings can be expressed or picked up by the therapist through their counter-transference. For example, with the case of the couple mentioned earlier, if the therapist has a similar fear of too much closeness, the therapist will feel themselves having feeling of anger like the wife has for the husband. If the therapist resembles the husband and is desirous of intimate partner talks in their own life, the therapist will feel anger at the wife. These are feelings that are disowned by the client, but which may be indicators that one of the primary defences is operating.

Solomon (1997) observed that for the therapist 'the reception of one or both partners' unwanted affectivity could become the basis for pathological collusions or a tool for empathic understanding' (p. 27). She went on to focus on two types of counter-transference: (1) concordant counter-transference if the therapist feels angry when a wife describes in a flat and unperturbed manner the severe abuse she suffered at the hands of her husband; and (2) complementary counter-transference, the therapist taking on temporarily the role and the feelings of the parent or spouse in regard to a client.

First, if a client has a critical parent the therapist can find themselves feeling critical of the patient in ways not usually felt with other patients. This is a very sophisticated use of therapist self-awareness. With one or more people in a session this process becomes more complex and challenging. Second, for some patients their whole self and personality is fashioned around pleasing and accommodating to the people in their immediate environment (Lee, 2000).

Some children have the burden of functioning as self-objects for their parents instead of vice versa. In order to keep cohesive a parent on whom they depend for survival, they de-centre from their own developmental needs and feelings. As adults these people tend to find partners who fill the same niche as their parents. They have a well-developed peripheral self and an underdeveloped core self, which lacks idealised values, associated goals, purposes and ambitions that mobilise self-assertiveness. As with their parents, they struggle to keep their partner's emotions stable and predictable and to bolster their shaky self-esteem. An example of this would be in marriages in which women accommodate to their male partners' political opinions because their husbands are insecure and cannot tolerate any other points of view.

Many authors have discussed the role of these children as reverse self-objects or, in family therapy terminology, parentified children. Lee (1999) noted

> Mutuality helps the infant energise the mother who in turn continues her investment in the infant. Under such a model, what is traumatic is an infant's prolonged functioning as a self-object for a parent who has no capacity for mutuality, or has a significant temporary inability to respond. The infant's self-object function for the parent becomes exhausting, burdensome, and then traumatic, without reciprocal self-object experience with the parent ... As long as there is mutuality, an infant is able to function as a self-object for the parent without feeling exploited, enraged, or traumatised. (p. 180)

One couple (seen by a therapist in another country) was believed by family and friends to be the perfect couple. They had married very young. Both were serious, loving, responsible and dedicated parents, neighbours, co-workers and community members. Once their children left home they hit a rough spot and nearly broke up. On some level each of them had had enough of being the 'good child' — roles they had inherited from their families of origin.

- Her father had always been critical and told her she was not good enough (lack of mirroring self-object functioning) and she had never been able to stand up to her father. She vowed she would never be critical of her partner or children.

- He had never had to define himself in opposition to his incredibly supportive parents (lack of detailed mirroring a realistic feedback) and had modelled himself on his parents always accommodating and accepting others' views. On reflection he realised he felt his parents, if supportive, had left him in a psychological vacuum with insufficient guidance on how to judge his own preferences. He had always done his best in the marriage. He was totally surprised when his wife started saying she had had enough and felt stifled in the marriage to the point of wanting to leave.

- They realised that both of them had been reverse self-objects, keeping parents happy rather than being able to develop their own selves, their own goals within the marriage. Neither of them had ever fought for what they each wanted in their families of origin or with each other. The resentment towards each other merged with their family-of-origin issues.

Some of the general recommendations in working with couples include notions of regulation of emotion: dosage, containment, repair, balancing, tracking, responding out of the needed self-object transference, understanding, explaining and connecting to other aspects of experience (Kohut, 1984).

Livingston (1995, 1998) and Goldstein (1997) in their work with couples have emphasised the need to enable patients to drop their defences, including contempt and shame, and share their vulnerable selves in a safe and nurturing context, acknowledge individual and conflicting needs, provide an interpretation that includes both subjectivities, contain destructive behaviour by setting limits and providing structure, and then create a shared reality within which all parties can feel accepting and accepted.

During this process it is important to protect the couple and family members from invalidation by one another. Livingston (1995) He also pointed out that in therapy the couple doing this kind of hard work will need 'mirroring, respect and at times praise for the struggle involved' (p. 437). His comments evoke the awareness of the inflammable emotional interactivity of families. The challenge is for therapists to sit with it, follow it, make sense of it and manage it in ways that are productive but not destructive of processes in sessions and at home. I believe self-psychology opens up the inter-affective field for exploration. In particular, a focus on tracking breakdown emotions of anxiety and rage, and studying the reciprocity of the self-reflective feelings such as disgust, contempt, dismell and shame in different types of families is of interest.

The emphasis in this work is to channel the couple's communication to and through the therapist during the initial stages. This strategy contains their volatility until each partner feels sufficiently understood and validated in their emotions. After this is accomplished a therapist can encourage partners to speak directly to each other.

Experience helps. Over the years I have drawn on and used various theoretical perspectives. I will indulge myself in an attempt to bridge a debate in the field. Although Schnarch (1997) is scathing in his criticism of empathy-based therapies, it is my contention that people who work from the analytic perspective of self-psychology would not have any qualms about adopting his definition of a mature and differentiated couple relationship. In such a relationship both partners are able to articulate and regulate their own emotional states. They remain intimate yet firm in their respective selves in the presence of one another, and provide each other with mature self-object functions. To illustrate this I quote Schnarch's definition of his elaboration of Bowen's (1988) concept of differentiation, namely hanging on to yourself and being self-validating:

> In a nutshell, differentiation is the process by which we become more uniquely ourselves by maintaining ourselves in relationship with those we love ... differentiation is the key to not holding grudges and recovering quickly from arguments, to tolerating intense intimacy and maintaining your priorities in the midst of your everyday life. (p. 51)

> Differentiation is the ability to maintain your sense of self when your partner is away or when you are not in a primary love relationship ... Highly differentiated people can be heedful of their impact on others and take their partners' needs and priorities into account ... The differentiated self is solid but permeable, allowing you to remain close even when your partner tries to mould or manipulate you. When you have a solid core of values or beliefs, you can change without losing your identity. (p. 67)

> Differentiation is not about putting yourself ahead of everyone else. You can choose to be guided by your partner's best interests, even at the price of your individual agenda. But it does not leave

you feeling like you're being ruled by someone else's needs ...
What they want for themselves becomes as important to you as
what you want for yourself ... What I am describing is called
mutuality. When you participate in the agendas of those you love
and sacrifice out of your own differentiation, it enhances your self-
esteem rather than leaving you feeling like you have sold yourself
out. (p. 68)

The goal is to help each person develop a more cohesive, vital
and articulated sense of self, have more flexible and positive
self-organising principles, and ultimately to help each to eventually develop the skill of having 'a self and being able to
empathise simultaneously' with another intimate person. This
phrase, used by a patient of Shaddock's (2000), I believe very
aptly captures the essence of Schnarch's (1997) concept of self-
differentiation. Self-differentiation is a case of focusing on the
conjunction of 'me and you', rather than either 'me or you'. This
means that 'doing something your way because you want it'
results in a loss of self and ultimately impoverishes the relationship. If I choose to go my partner's way, I do so willingly
without resentment. Each partner is able to be fully him- or
herself, and to be able to remain connected to the other without
sacrificing any vital part of their individuality. This is difficult
for narcissistically vulnerable people, and for all of us in certain
areas. The goal is a good relationship with self alongside a good
relationship with a chosen, significant other, as well as the
strengthening of self-object functions in the present and hopefully for patients' future lives (Kohut, 1971, 1984).

This type of couple relationship is the bedrock for healthy family
relationships and the raising of vitally alive, emotionally expressive and empathic, flexible, creative, wise, warmly engaging and
securely attached children (Kohut, 1974).

Family-of-Origin scale

Severely dysfunctional family (scale 1–2)

This family is characterised by multi-generational patterns of emotional dysfunction. In the generations there are a number (at least three) of the following:

- Serious mental illness of a psychotic nature such as schizophrenia or manic-depressive illness.
- Violence in relationships, physical abuse and deprivation which affects children.
- Suicides in more than one generation.
- Incest and child sexual abuse.
- Alcoholism and other addictions such as gambling.
- Criminal behaviour.
- Eating disorders such as anorexia or bulimia.
- Relationships marked by emotional turbulence with most ending in divorce, or unstable de facto relationships, affairs.
- The level of occupational functioning may be quite low with numerous people on invalid and unemployed pensions.
- Trauma such as war with migration. (Scale 1–2 for poor–moderate within this range.)

Dysfunctional family (scale 3–5)

This family is characterised by one of the above serious themes in the nuclear family-of-origin (include blended, single parent, etc.) and this theme tends to dominate interpersonal interaction (eg., alcoholism and co-dependency). This pattern may or may not be an intergenerational pattern. Relationships tend to be marked by reactivity and turbulence, most marriages within the wider family tending to end with separation and divorce. Verbal abuse and in some cases violence may be part of the family history. (Scale 3–5 for poor–moderate–high within this range.)

Normal range family (scale 6–8)

There is obviously a large range of what might be labelled normal. There may be signs of distress such as depression, anxiety or stress among members of the family. The marital relationship may have some distress and conflict, but there is at least the capacity to discuss it to some degree. There are unconscious relationship factors such as projection (blaming another person for personal issues). Triangles may be dysfunctional. There may be some difficulty handling emotions and expressing affection. Values are important. The 'bread-winners' tend to have jobs and there is money for essentials. (Scale 6–8 for low–moderate–high within this range.)

High functioning family (scale 9–10)

These families are characterised by open communication, individuals relate with intimacy and mutual support. There is a sense of connection. Relationships tend to be more conscious than unconscious so individuals will ask for what is wanted. Stable relationships are the norm in the wider family. People tend to be successful in their careers (hopefully without workaholism). Decisions are shaped by values and principles and if there are spiritual values they are well integrated into the family. (Scale 9-10 for superior–very superior in this range.)

Murray Bowen (1972) developed a scale of self-differentiation. It is with his principles in mind that I have attempted to make this scale of functioning in the family-of-origin. The scale is hardly precise, instead it is a general guideline for the level of functioning in families.

Reflect

Compare this scale with the Global Assesement of Functioning (GAF) scale (for individuals) in the *Diagnostic and Statistical Manual of Mental Disorders* (DSM-IV). How would you assess your family-of-origin on this measure?

1. For an overview of the history of couple counselling see Gurman A., & Fraenckel, P. (2002), The history of couple therapy: A millennial review, *Family Process*, 42(2), 199–260. For M. White (1987), Couple therapy: 'Urgency for Sameness' or 'Appreciation of Difference', *Dulwich Review*, Summer, 11–13. See the collection of papers 'Experience, contradiction, narrative, and imagination' by D. Epston and M. White (1992), South Australia: Dulwich Centre Publications. Also Arnstein, M. (1988), An overview of three models of marital therapy, *The Australian and New Zealand Journal of Family Therapy*, 9(3), 151–158. I wrote a paper on thinking about chaos theory and systems: Stevens, B. (1991), Chaos: A challenge to refine systems theory, *Australia and New Zealand Journal of Family Therapy*, 12(1), 23–26. Cf. Gottman (1999) has mentioned attractors in relationships, p. 37.

2. Malise sees this person as having more power, in terms of presentation, he or she will have less need of the relationship.

3. Bishop Ian George (then Archdeacon) developed a pre-marriage course at St Johns Anglican Church, Reid in Canberra in the 1980's.

4. Note how many of the standard skills taught in clinical psychology programs are useful at this point — for example, breathing, countering negative and catastrophic thinking, visualisation of a safe place, noticing areas of tension in the body and stress reduction strategies. Biofeedback may also be used.

5. There is considerable research on the 'high conflict family' and how this can affect children: Garrity C., & Baris, M. (1994), *Caught in the middle: Protecting the children of high conflict divorce*, San Francisco: Josey Bass; Johnston, J., & Roseby, V. (1997), *In the name of the child: A developmental approach to understanding and helping children of conflicted and violent divorce*, New York: The Free Press. The goal is to move towards co-operative parenting, and their characteristics are seen in Ehrenberg, M. (1996), Cooperative parenting arrangements after marital separation: Former couples who make it work, *Journal of Divorce and Remarriage*, 26(1/2), 93–115.

6. In Australia, start with The Institute for Emotion Focused Therapy in Sydney. See www.EFTherapy.com

7. When a relationship is happy, other potential relationships do not look attractive or seem unduly risky and costly. If the relationship is failing then other relationships start looking good (Gottman, 1999, p. 73)

8. Research of L. Gigy and J. Kelly of the California Divorce Mediation Project, cited by Gottman, 1999, p. 23.

9. Paradoxically an affair can stimulate sexual activity and increase satisfaction.

10. Freud, 1914/1963, in his important paper 'On narcissism: An introduction', referred to primitive aspects of personality with a 'megalomania, an over-estimation of the power of wishes and an "omnipotence of thoughts"'. See *General psychological theory*, New York: Collier Books, p. 58. Kohut, H. (1971), *The analysis of the self*, Madison, CN: International Universities Press, pp. 3–4; Kernberg, O. (1986), Further contributions, in A. Morrison (Ed.), *Essential papers on narcissism* (p. 252), New York: New York Universities Press.

11. Dan Wile, in *After the honeymoon*, cited in Gottman and Silver, 1999, p. 131.

12. Based on papers presented at the Australian Family Therapy Conference, Adelaide, SA, October 2003 and, at the Empathink Summer School in Canberra 2009. I thank Tom Young (2003) for reminding me of Stern's (1985) term 'inter-affectivity'.

Abrams Spring, J. (1996). *After the affair: Healing the pain and rebuilding trust when a partner has been unfaithful.* New York: Harper Collins.

Ackerman, N.A. (1966). *Treating the troubled family.* New York: Basic Books.

American Psychological Association. (2002). Criteria for evaluating treatment guidelines. *American Psychologist, 57,* 1052–1059.

American Psychological Association Presidential Task Force on Evidence-Based Practice. (2006). *Evidence-based practice in psychology.* Retrieved from http://www.apa.org/practice/ebpreport.pdf

Anonymous. (1972). Toward the differentiation of a self in one's own family [Bowen, M.]. In J. Framo (Ed.), *Family interaction: A dialogue between family researchers and family therapists.* (pp: 111–173). New York: Springer.

Annon, J. (1976). *Behavioral treatment of sexual problems (the PLISSIT Model)* (Vols. 1–2). New York: Harper & Row.

Arnstein, M. (1988). An overview of three models of marital therapy. *Australian and New Zealand Journal of Family Therapy, 9*(3), 151–158.

Arnstein, M. (2003, September). *What can self-psychology offer family therapists? Building blocks for a focus on family inter-affectivity.* Paper presented at the Australian Family Therapy Conference, Adelaide, South Australia.

Arnstein, M. (2009, January). *You, me and us: What couple and family therapy can offer individual therapists.* Paper presented at the Empathink Summer School, ANU, Canberra, ACT, Australia.

Banks, G. (1981). *Helping your child through separation and divorce.* Melbourne, Australia: Dove Communications.

Barnish, M. (2004). *Domestic violence: A literature review.* HM Inspectorate of Probation. Retrieved from www.homeoffice.gov.uk/justice/probation/insp-prob/index.html

Basch, M.F. (1992). *Practicing psychotherapy: A casebook.* New York: Basic Books.

Baucom, D.H., & Epstein, N. (1990). *Cognitive-behavioral marital therapy.* Levittown, PA: Brunner/Mazel.

Bayley, L., & Lee, R. (2002, January). *Mother–daughter envy.* Paper presented at the Empathink Seminar, Melbourne, Australia.

Berman, J., & Berman, L. (2001). *For women only: A revolutionary guide to reclaiming your sex life.* London: Virago.

Bernal, G., & Baker, J. (1979). Towards a meta-communicational framework of couple interactions. *Family Process, 18,* 293–302.

Bograd, M., & Mederos, F. (1999). Battering and couples therapy: Universal screening and selection of treatment modality. *Journal of Marital and Family Therapy, 25*(3), 291–312.

Boscolo, L., Cecchin, G., Hoffman, L., & Papp, P. (1987). *Milan systemic family therapy.* New York: Basic Books.

Bowen, M. (1988). *Family therapy in clinical practice.* London: Aronson.

Bowlby, J. (1969, 1973, 1980) *Attachment and loss.* Vols. 1–3. New York: Basic Books.

Boszormenyi-Nagy, I. & Ulrich, D.N., 1981. Contextual family therapy. In A.S. Gurman & D.P. Kniskern (Eds.), *Handbook of family therapy* (pp. 159–186). New York: Brunner/Mazel.

Brighton-Cleghorn, J. (1987). Formulations of self and family systems. *Family Process, 26,* 185–201.

Bray, J. (2010, July). *Family psychology and therapy: Advances in treatment of couples and families.* Keynote address presented to the 27th International Congress of Applied Psychology, Melbourne, Australia.

Broderick, C.B., & Schrader, S.S. (1981). The history of professional marriage and family therapy. In A.S. Gurman & D.P. Kniskern (Eds.), *Handbook of family therapy* (pp. 5–32). New York: Brunner and Mazel.

Brown, E.M. (1991). *Patterns of infidelity and their treatment.* New York: Brunner/Mazel.

Brown, J. (2007). Therapy with same sex couple: Guidelines for embracing the subjugated discourse; also Challenging the stereotypes of gay male and lesbian couples: A research perspective. In E. Shaw & J. Crawley (Eds.), *Couple therapy in Australia: Issues emerging from practice.* Melbourne, Australia: PsychOz.

Brown, N. (2003). *Loving the self-absorbed: How to create a more satisfying relationship with a narcissistic partner.* Oakland, CA: New Harbinger Publications.

Buber, M. (1937, 2004). *I and thou.* London: Continuum.

Burch, B., & Jenkins, C. (1999). The interactive potential between individual therapy and couple therapy: An intersubjective paradigm. *Contemporary Psychoanalysis, 35,* 229–252.

Capaldi, D.M., & Kim, H.K. (2007). Typological approaches to violence in couples and alternative conceptual approach. *Clinical Psychology Review, 27*(3), 253–265.

Carnes, P., Delmonico, D.L., & Griffin, E. (2007). *In the shadows of the net center city.* Center City, MN: Hazelden.

Coontz, S. (2006). *Marriage, a history: How love conquered marriage.* New York: Penguin Books.

Covey, S. (1990). *The seven habits of highly effective people: Restoring the character ethic.* Melbourne, Australia: The Business Library.

Crawley, J. (1998). Couples therapy: Unravelling the strands. *Australian and New Zealand Journal of Family Therapy, 19*(4), 167–177.

Crawley, J., & Grant, J. (2002). *Attachment theory, couples therapy & EFT.* Paper presented at the Melbourne Psychotherapy in Australia Conference.

Damasio. A. (2000). *The feeling of what happens: Body, emotion and the making of consciousness.* Reading and Berkshire: Vintage Books.

Donaldson-Pressman, S., & Pressman R. (1994). *The narcissistic family: Diagnosis and treatment*. New York: Lexington Books.

Fisher, B. (1992). *Rebuilding: When your relationship ends* (2nd ed.). San Luis Obispo, CA: Impact Publishers.

Flaskas, C. (1994). Exploring the therapeutic relationship: A case study. *Australian and New Zealand Journal of Family Therapy. 15*(4), 185–190.

Fogarty, T. (1976). Systems, concepts and the dimensions of the self. In P.J. Guerin Jr. (Ed.), *Family therapy* (pp. 144–153). New York: Gardner Press.

Fonagy, P. (2008). A genuinely developmental theory of sexual enjoyment and its implication for psychoanalytic technique. *Journal of the American Psychoanalytic Association, 56*(1), 11–36.

Fonagy, P., Steele, M., Higgitt, A., & Target. M. (1994). Theory and practice of resilience. *Journal of Child Psychology and Psychiatry, 35*, 231–257.

Framo, J.L. (1982). *Explorations in marital and family therapy*. Selected papers of James Framo, New York: Springer.

Friedman, E. (1985). *Generation to generation*. New York: Guilford Press.

Gibney, P. (2003). *The pragmatics of therapeutic practice*. Melbourne, Australia: PsychOz Publications.

Goldberg, J. (1993). *The dark side of love: The positive role of our negative feelings — anger, jealousy and hate*. London: Aquarian/Thorsons.

Greenberg, L.S., & Goldman, R.N. (2008). *Emotion-focussed couples therapy: The dynamics of emtion, love and power*. Washington: American Psychological Association.

Goldner, V. (1998). The treatment of violence and victimization in intimate relationships. *Family Process, 37*(3), 263–286.

Goldstein, E.G. (1997). Counter-transference reactions to borderline couples. In M.F. Solomon & J.P. Siegel (Eds.), *Counter transference in couples therapy*. New York: Norton.

Gordon, K.C., & Baucom, D.H. (1988). Understanding betrayal in marriage: A synthesised model of forgiveness. *Family Process, 37*(4), 425–449.

Gordon, R.G. (1987, October). *Faces of intimacy: The role of intimate affect in the structure of the self*. Paper presented at the Annual Self Psychology Conference in Chicago.

Gottman, J.M. (1999). *The marriage clinic: A scientifically based marital therapy*. New York: W.W. Norton.

Gottman, J.M., & Silver, N. (1999). *The seven principles for making your marriage work*. New York: Three Rivers Press.

Gottmann, J., & Jacobsen, N. (1998). *Breaking the cycle: New insights into violent relationships*. London: Bloomsbury.

Grant, A., Townend, M., Mills, J., & Cockx, A. (2009). *Assessment and case formulation in cognitive behavioural therapy*. London: Sage.

Granvold, D. (1983). Structured separation for marital treatment and decision-making. *Journal of Marital and Family Therapy, 9*(4), 403–412.

Greenberg, L.S. & Johnson, S.M. (1988). *Emotionally focused therapy for couples*. New York: Guilford Press.

Greenberg, L.S., & Goldman, R.N. (2008). *Emotionally focused couples therapy: The dynamics of emotion, love and power.* Washington, DC: American Psychological Association.

Greenspan, S.I. (1999). *Developmentally based psychotherapy.* Madison, CT: International University Press.

Guerin, P. Jr., Fay, L.F., Burden, S.L., & Kautto, J.G. (1987). *The evaluation and treatment of marital conflict: A four-stage approach.* New York: Basic Books.

Gurman, A.S., & Fraenckel, P. (2002). The history of couple therapy: A millennial review. *Family Process, 41*(2), 199–260.

Haidt, J. (2001). The emotional dog and its rational tail: A social intuitionist approach to moral judgment. *Psychological Review, 108,* 813–834.

Haidt, J. (2003). The moral emotions. In R.J. Davidson, K.R. Scherer & H.H. Goldsmith (Eds.), *The handbook of affective sciences* (pp. 852–870). New York: Oxford University Press.

Halford, W.K., Kelly, A., & Markman, H.J. (1997). The concept of a happy marriage. In W.K. Halford and H.J. Markman (Eds.), *Clinical handbook of marriage and couples intervention* (pp. 3–9). Chichester, England: John Wiley & Sons Ltd.

Halford, W.K., Markman, H.J., Kling, G.H., & Stanley, S.M. (2007). Best practice in couple relationship education. *Journal of Marital and Family Therapy, 29*(3), 385–406.

Hamel, J. (2005). *Gender inclusive Treatment of intimate partner abuse: A comprehensive approach.* New York: Springer.

Harris, R. (2009). *ACT with love: Stop struggling, reconcile differences, and strengthen your relationship with acceptance and commitment therapy.* Oakland, CA: New Harbinger.

Hayes, H. (1990). Marital therapy: The therapist. *Australian and New Zealand Journal of Family Therapy, 11*(2), 96–103.

Haynes, J.M. (1981). *Divorce mediation.* New York: Springer.

Heiman J., & LoPiccolo, J. (1988, first published 1976). *Becoming orgasmic: A sexual growth programme for women.* New York: Prentice Hall.

Hendrix, H. (1988). *Getting the love you want: A guide for couples.* New York: Henry Holt.

Heru, A.M. (2007). Intimate partner violence: Treating abuser and abused. *Advances in Psychiatric Treatment, 13,* 376–383.

Hubble, M.A., Duncan, B.L., & Miller, S.D. (1999). *The heart and soul of change.* Washington, DC: American Psychological Association.

Jacobson, N.S., & Christensen, A. (1996). *Integrative couple therapy: Promoting acceptance and change.* New York: W.W. Norton.

Jacobson, N.S., & Margolin, G. (1979). *Marital therapy: Strategies based on social learning and behavior exchange principles.* New York: Brunner/Mazel.

Jansen, D., & Newman, M. (1989). *Really relating: How to build an enduring relationship,* Sydney: Hutchinson.

Jenkins, A. (1990). *Invitations to responsibility: The therapeutic engagement of men who are violent and abusive.* Adelaide, South Australia: Dulwich Centre Publications.

Johnson, S.M. (1996). *The practice of emotionally focussed marital therapy: Creating connection.* New York: Brunner/Mazel.

Johnson, S.M. (2002). *Emotionally focused couple therapy with trauma survivors: Strengthening attachment bonds.* New York: The Guilford Press.

Johnson, S.M. (2004). *The practice of emotionally focused couple therapy: Creating connection* (2nd ed.). New York: Brunner-Routledge.

Johnson, S., & Lebow, J. (2000). The 'coming of age' of couple therapy: A decade review. *Journal of Marital and Family Therapy, 26,* 23–38.

Johnson, S.M., & Whiffen, V.E. (1999). Made to measure: Adapting emotionally focused therapy to partners' attachment styles. *Clinical Psychology: Science and Practice, 6*(4), 366–381.

Jory, B. (2004). The Intimate Justice Scale: An instrument to screen for psychological abuse and physical violence in clinical practice. *Journal of Marital and Family Therapy, 30*(1), 29–44.

Kalter, N. (1990). *Growing up with divorce: Helping your child avoid immediate and later emotional problems.* New York: Free Press.

Kashack, E., & Tiefer, L. (2002). *A new view of women's sexual problems.* New York: Haworth.

Kaslow, F. (1981). Divorce and divorce therapy. In A. Gurman & D. Kniskern, (Eds.), *Handbook of family therapy.* New York: Brunner Mazel.

Kelly, J., & Johnson, M. (2008). *Family Court Review, 46*(3), 476–499.

Kerr, M.E. (1981). Family systems theory and therapy. In A.S. Gurman & D.P. Kniskern, (Eds.), *Handbook of family therapy,* New York: Brunner/Mazel.

Kerr, M.E. (1984). Theoretical base for differentiation of self in one's family of origin. In C.E. Munson (Ed.), *Family of origin applications in clinical supervision.* New York: Hawthorn Press.

Kerr, M.E. (1988). *Family evaluation: An approach based on Bowen theory.* New York: W.W. Norton and Company.

King, R. (1998). *Good loving, great sex.* Sydney, Australia: Random House.

King, R. (1999). *The sexual counselling workbook.* Sydney, Australia: The Written Word.

Kohut, H. (1971). *The analysis of the self.* New York: International Universities Press.

Kohut, H. (1977). *The restoration of the self.* New York: International Universities Press.

Kohut, H. (1984). *How does analysis cure?* A. Goldberg, (Ed.). Chicago: University of Chicago Press.

Kohut, H. (1996, his lecture was in 1974). The mature transformations of narcissism. In P. Tolpin & M. Tolpin (Eds.), *Heinz Kohut — The Chicago Institute lectures* (pp. 79–92). Hillsdale, NJ: The Analytic Press.

Kohut, H., & Wolf, E. (1978). The disorders of the self and their treatment: An outline. *International Journal of Psycho-Analysis, 59,* 413–425.

Lachman, F., & Beebe, B., (1999). The contribution of self and mutual regulation to therapeutic action: A case illustration. In J. Cassidy & P. Shaver, (Eds.), *Handbook of attachment* (p. 575). New York: Guilford Press.

Lawson, A. (1988). *Adultery: An analysis of love and betrayal.* New York: Basic Books.

Lebow, J. (1997). The integrative revolution in couple and family therapy. *Family Process, 36*(1), 1–17.

LeDoux, J. (1996). *The emotional brain: The mysterious underpinnings of emotional life.* New York: Touchstone Books, Simon & Schuster.

Lee, R.R. (1998). Empathy and affects: Towards an inter-subjective view. *Australian Journal of Psychotherapy, 17,* 127–149.

Lee, R.R. (1999). An infant's experience as self-object. *American Journal of Psychotherapy, 53*(2), 177–187.

Lee, R.R. (2000). *Psychotherapy after Tomkins: A textbook on evolutionary affect theory.* Unpublished paper.

Leone, C. M. (2001). Towards a more optimal self-object milieu: Family psychotherapy from the perspective of self psychology. *Clinical Social Work Journal, 29*(3), 269–289.

Lerner, H. (1985). *The dance of anger.* New York: Harper and Row.

Lerner, H. (1989). *The dance of intimacy.* New York: Harper and Row.

Lewis. M. (1992). *Shame: The exposed self.* New York: The Free Press.

Lieblum, S. (Ed.). (2007). *The principles and practice of sex therapy* (4th ed.). New York: The Guilford Press.

Linehan, M.M. (1993). *Cognitive-behavioral treatment of borderline personality disorder.* New York: Guilford Press.

Livingston, M. (1995). A self psychologist in couples land: Multi subjective approach to transference and counter-transference-like phenomena in marital relationship. *Family Process, 24*(4), 427–440.

Livingston, M. (1998). Conflict and aggression in couples therapy: A self-psychological vantage point. *Family Process, 37*(3), 300–311.

Mace, D. (1948). *Marriage counselling.* London: Churchill.

Magai, C. (1999). Affect, imagery and attachment: Working models of interpersonal affect and the socialisation of emotion. In J. Cassidy & P. Shaver (Eds.), *Handbook of attachment.* New York: Guilford Press.

MacKinnon, L. & James, K. (1987). Theory and practice of the Milan systemic approach. *Australian and New Zealand Journal of Family Therapy, 8*(2), 89–98.

McCormack, C. (1989). The borderline/schizoid marriage: The holding environment as an essential treatment construct. *Journal of Marital and Family Therapy, 15*(3), 299–309.

McCormack, C. (2000). *Treating borderline states in marriage.* Northvale, NJ: Jason Aronson, Northvale.

McEwan, I. (2007). *On Chesil beach.* London: John Cape.

McGoldrick, M., & Gerson, R. (1985). *Genograms in family assessment.* New York: W.W. Norton.

McWilliams, N. (1994). *Psychoanalytic diagnosis: Understanding personality structure in the clinical process.* New York: Guilford Press.

McWilliams, N. (1999). *Psychoanalytic case formulation.* New York: Guilford Press.

Meichenbaum, D. (2007). *Family violence: Treatment of perpetrators and victims,* www.melissainstitute.org

Miller, G. & de Shazer, S. (1998). Have you heard the latest rumor about...? Solution focussed therapy as a rumor. *Family Process, 37,* 363–377.

Moir, A., & Jessel, D. (1989). *Brain sex.* London: Mandarin.

Ogden, T. (1999). The analytic third: Working with intersubjective clinical facts. In S. Mitchell and L. Aaron (Eds.), *Relational psychoanalysis: The emergence of a tradition* (pp. 459–492). Hillsdale, NJ: The Analytic Press.

Panksepp, J. (1998). *Affective neuroscience: The foundation of human and animal emotions.* New York: Oxford University Press.

Peck, M.S. (2002). *The road less travelled: A new psychology of love, traditional values and spiritual growth.* New York: Simon and Schuster.

Perry, R. (1993). Empathy — still at the heart of therapy. *Australian and New Zealand Journal of Family Therapy, 14*(2), 63–74.

Pinker, S. (2002). *The blank slate: The modern denial of human nature.* London, England: Penguin.

Pinsof, W.M., & Wynne, L.C. (1995). The effectiveness of marital and family therapy: An empirical overview, conclusions and recommendations. *Journal of Marital and Family Therapy, 21*(4), 341–343.

Relate Institute. (2011). Retrieved from https://www.relate-institute.org/

Ringstrom, P. (1994). An inter-subjective approach to conjoint therapy. *Progress in Self Psychology, 10,* 159–182.

Rowe, C.E. Jr., & Mac Isaac, D.S. (1991). *Empathic atunement: The technique of psychoanalytic self psychology.* Northvale, NJ: Jason Aronson.

Sager, C. (1981). Couples therapy and marriage contracts. In A. Gurman & D. Kniskern (Eds.), *Handbook of family therapy* (pp. 85–130). New York: Brunner and Mazel.

Schnarch, D. (1997). *Passionate marriage: keeping love and intimacy alive in committed relationships.* London: W.W. Norton.

Schnarch, D. (2002). *Resurrecting sex: Resolving sexual problems and rejuvenating your relationship.* Melbourne, Australia: Scribe Press.

Schore, A. (1994). *Affect regulation and the origins of the self,* Hillsdale, NJ: Erlbaum.

Schore, A. (1997). Interdisciplinary developmental research as a source of clinical models. In M. Moskowits, C. Monk, K. Kaye & S.J. Ellman (Eds.), *The neurobiological and developmental basis for psychotherapeutic intervention.* Northvale, NJ: Jason Aronson.

Scheff, T.J. (1994). *Bloody revenge: Emotions, nationalism and war.* Boulder, CO: Westview Press.

Sexton, T.L., & Gordon, K.C. (2009). Science, practice, and evidence-based treatments in the clinical practice of family psychology. In J.H. Bray & M.

Stanton (Eds.), *The Wiley-Blackwell handbook of family psychology* (pp. 314–326). Malden, MA: Wiley-Blackwell.

Shaddock, D. (2000). *Contexts and connections: An inter-subjective systems approach to couples therapy.* New York: Basic Books.

Shapiro, F. (1995). *Eye movement desensitisation and reprocessing: Basic principles, protocols and procedures.* New York: Guilford Press.

Shapiro, S. (1984). *Manhood: A new definition.* New York: G.P. Putnam's Sons.

Siegel, D.J., (1999). *The developing mind: Toward a neurobiology of interpersonal experience.* New York: Guilford Press.

Smith, J., Osmam., & Goding, M. (1990). Reclaiming the emotional aspects of the therapist-family system. *Australian and New Zealand Journal of Family Therapy, 11*(3), 140–146.

Smith, M. I. (1975). *When I say no, I feel guilty.* New York: Dial Press.

Socarides, D., & Stolorow, R.D. (1984). Affects and self objects. *Annual of Psychoanalysis* (Vol. 12). New York: International University Press.

Solomon, M.F. (1989). *Narcissism and intimacy: Love and marriage in an age of confusion.* New York: W.W. Norton.

Solomon, M.F. (1997). Counter-transference and empathy in couples therapy. In M.F. Solomon & J.P. Siegel (Eds.), *Counter transference in couples therapy.* New York: Norton.

Spring, J.A. (1996). *After the affair: Healing the pain and rebuilding trust when a partner has been unfaithful.* New York: Perennial Harper Collins.

Stagoll, B., & Lang, M. (1980). Climbing the family tree: Working with genograms. *Australian Journal of Family Therapy, 1*(4), 161–170.

Stern, D.N. (1985). *The interpersonal world of the infant: A view from psychoanalysis and developmental psychology.* New York: Basic Books.

Stevens, B.A. (2001) *Mirror, mirror: When self-love undermines your relationship.* Melbourne, Australia: PsychOZ Publications.

Stevens, B.A. (2003, February). Impossible relationships. *Psychotherapy in Australia* [refereed section] 68–74.

Stith, S.M., Rosen, K.H., McCollum, E.E., & Thomsen, C.J. (2004). Treating intimate partner violence within intact couples relationships: Outcomes of multi-couple versus individual couple therapy. *Journal of Marital and Family Therapy, 30*(3), 305–318.

Stolorow, R.D., Brandshaft, B. & Atwood, G.E. (1995). *Psychoanalytic treatment: An intersubjective approach.* Hillsdale, NJ: The Analytic Press.

Strozier, C. B. (2001). *Heinz Kohut: The making of a psychoanalyst.* New York: Farrar, Straus and Giroux.

Stuart, R. (1980). *Helping couples change.* New York: Guilford Press.

Suskind, P. (1986). *Perfume: The story of a murderer.* London: Penguin Books.

Tolman, W. (1969). *Family constellation: Its effects on personality and social behaviour* (2nd ed.). New York: Springer.

Tolpin, P., & Tolpin, M., (1996). *Heinz Kohut: The Chicago Institute lectures.* Hillsdale, NJ: The Analytic Press.

Tomkins, S. (1962, 1963, 1991, 1992). *Affect, imagery and consciousness* (Vols. 1–4). New York: Springer.

von Bertalanffy, L. (1968). *General systems theory: Foundations, development, applications* (2nd ed.). New York: George Braziller.

Vygotsky, L.S. (1962). *Thought and language.* Cambridge, MA: MIT Press.

Wahba, R. (1991). Envy in the transference: Specific self-object disruption (Vol. 7). In A. Goldberg, (Ed.), *The evolution of self psychology: Progress in self psychology,* (pp. 137–154). Hillsdale, NJ: Analytic Press.

Walters, M., Carter, B., Papp, P., & Silverstein, O. (1988). *The invisible web: Gender patterns in family relationships.* New York: Guilford Press.

Watts, P. (2008). *Shared care or divided lives.* Canning Bridge, Australia: Ogilvie Publishing.

Watts, P. (2009). *Workshop: Understanding internet addiction.* Canberra, Australia.

Weeks, G.R., & Treat, S. (1992) *Couples in treatment.* New York: Brunner/Mazel.

Weiner-Davis, M. (2003, May–June). In the mood: Desire seldom comes to those who wait. *Psychotherapy Networker,* 32–35 and 56–57.

Werner, H. (1948 [1957 2nd ed.]). *The comparative psychology of mental development.* New York: International University Press.

White, M., & Epston, D. (1989). *Literate means to therapeutic ends.* Adelaide, Australia: Dulwich Centre Publications.

White, M., & Epston, D. (1990). *Narrative means to therapeutic ends.* New York: W.W. Norton.

Wolf, E.S. (1980). Developmental line of self-object relations. In A. Goldberg (Ed.), *Advances in self psychology* (pp. 117–130). New York: International University Press.

Wolf, E.S. (1993). Disruptions of the therapeutic relationship in psychoanalysis: A view from self psychology. *International Journal of Psycho-Analysis,* 74, 675–687.

Young, T.M. (2001). *Applying self psychology to psychotherapy with couples.* Unpublished manuscript. Available from Institute of Contemporary Psychotherapy, 4/4 Charles St, Petersham, Sydney, NSW, Australia, 2049.

Zilbergeld, B. (1999). *The new male sexuality* (2nd ed.). New York: Bantam Books.

www.ingramcontent.com/pod-product-compliance
Lightning Source LLC
Chambersburg PA
CBHW062030270326
41929CB00014B/2392